SYSTEM DESIGN INTERVIEW MADE EASY

DISCOVER 8 SIMPLE CASE STUDIES TO LEARN HOW TO PASS YOUR SYSTEM DESIGN INTERVIEW EASILY

RICHARD LEE

CONTENTS

INTRODUCTION

The development of software and services that not only offer knowledge, enrichment, and entertainment but also simplify daily life has been made possible by computers, which have also changed the world. It would have been completely normal for people to dismiss the idea of the internet changing lives at the dawn of the twenty-first century as nothing more than a theory. But twenty years later, the internet has taken over the world, and here we are. People use the internet to communicate, to express their opinions on social media platforms, to make thousands of dollars worth of purchases through e-commerce sites, and to spend a lot of time binge-watching TV shows that are streaming online.

Every application can be used by anyone and is made to be simple to use with the help of computers or smartphone. Although these applications are simple to use, they are maintained by systems that are complex and challenging to construct.

System design experts are a type of computer specialists who work on developing highly consistent and reliable systems. Popular computer studies like system design can show us how to scale our hardware resources for a given service.

WHO AM I?

I'm Richard Lee, a system design professional who has helped numerous businesses develop systems that maximize their offerings. When I was first learning to program, distributed systems captured my attention. I spent hours conducting my own research to determine the elements that enable the services because I was so interested in how a web application or mobile application would function.

I have mastered and have command over even complex system designs after many years of hard work and dedication. I worked with dozens of businesses to develop system designs that were scaled for their target markets. My passion for system design has enabled me to travel the world and connect with experts who have decades of experience scaling and distributing systems to prevent bottleneck situations.

Sysadmins were very impressed with my subject knowledge and ability to teach any complex topics in simple terms a few years ago when I was at a conference. Some of them inspired me to write a book that will enable enthusiasts or laypeople looking to land a job in system design. This idea initially made me hesitant because it can be challenging to explain intricate system design concepts in the context of a job interview for any of the well-known services.

But this idea has challenged me, and I was finally prepared to begin writing my book after months of thorough research. The book not only focuses on concepts but also offers real-world examples to help the reader comprehend the fundamentals more clearly. This book is certain to be interesting, informed, and helpful to readers who are passionate about system design but are unsure of the approaches they can take.

WHY SHOULD YOU READ THIS BOOK?

The software sector is at an all-time high, even in times of a global pandemic. Many business owners are using sophisticated computers that can carry out tasks for them to recreate their visions. In the software industry, there are currently countless applications and domains, ranging from e-commerce shopping to augmented reality. The field of system design has a promising future, and this book is a must-read for anyone interested in distributed systems.

Because you don't have to implement every functionality yourself as a system design expert, it differs significantly from programming. As an architect, you should be aware of every little detail that contributes to the strength of distributed systems. System design and architecture are quite similar.

Because system design is partly theoretical, it's important to understand some fundamental ideas that are involved in the backend operations of running applications, whether they are mobile or web-based. Experts predict that by 2030, computer-related technologies will directly affect more than half of the global economy. There has never been a better time than the present to master system design. You can push your knowledge beyond what is necessary to get a job in this field with the help of this book.

HOW SHOULD YOU READ THIS BOOK?

This book is more than just a list of interview questions and their associated answers. Interviews for system design don't go like that. In a system design interview, the interviewer will typically ask the candidate questions, and the candidate will then develop a design based on his or her responses.

Consider yourself in the circumstances before reading any of the case studies mentioned in this book. In our case studies, we followed the same format, which is typical for system design interviews where the conversation must flow naturally.

Utilize cognitive strategies like mind maps to help you remember the challenging material so you can get the most out of this book. For a better understanding of the service you are attempting to implement, take a look at the architecture diagrams offered for each case study.

We are eager to enlist your participation in a journey that could change your career and pique your interest in sophisticated computer systems.

So, first of all, thank you for purchasing this book. I know you could have picked any number of books to read, but you picked this book and for that I am extremely grateful.

I hope that it added at value and quality to your everyday life.

If you will enjoy this book and find some benefit in reading this, I'd like to hear from you and hope that you could take some time to post a review on Amazon. Your feedback and support will help this author to greatly improve his writing craft for future projects and make this book even better.

I want you, the reader, to know that your review is very important and so, if you'd like to leave a review, all you have to do is to scan the QR code and away you go.

I wish you all the best in your future success!

CHAPTER 1
INTRODUCTION TO SYSTEM DESIGN

An expert in distributed systems will comprehend the service and its functionalities to develop a logical blueprint for scaling the service for millions of users. System design is a field of computer science. Without scaling the hardware architecture to meet demand, you cannot please your audience.

Service outages can be a nightmare for businesses. To guarantee that the service is always available online, businesses can create and initialize cutting-edge computer components with the assistance of a system design expert.

Any distributed system can be scaled to meet an organization's objectives. The information in this chapter will be crucial for a beginner to comprehend the case studies discussed in this book.

HORIZONTAL SCALING VERSUS VERTICAL SCALING

Businesses expand over time. It is crucial for the founders of these services to scale their systems as their businesses expand in order to prevent downtime. Applications are powerful, usable, and addictive due to their scalability. The capacity of a system for handling requests is commonly referred to as scalability.

You should be aware of two scaling technologies that experts strongly advise for businesses that are just starting to grow or have the potential to get bigger in the future if you are fascinated by internet technologies and the business that surrounds them.

It is crucial for you to comprehend scalabilities as a system design professional and ways to combat them while developing solutions for the businesses or services you will work for that will change the industry.

What Is Scalability?

User requests are typically sent to the systems that support the services. A database server's connected applications are all limited to a certain number of requests per second. The application will stop functioning if any request exceeds its capacity because it is unable to handle any additional requests. The scalability limit refers to the systems' inability to perform tasks beyond their capabilities.

Every time a system is designed, the developers must project its scalability, or the number of requests one or all of the servers combined can handle, in order to enhance their services. No matter how effective your resources are, if they can only handle X requests but 'X+1' requests come in, they won't be able to handle them and the users sending requests to access your service risk having their access to it cut off.

How to Scale Machines?

Scaling your hardware resources requires efficient software management system redesign or the addition of new resources. You can use either of the two widely used approaches in the software industry to help your business expand. Businesses must scale if they want to lower latency and boost service availability. It is crucial for system designers to comprehend the service and choose which of the two scaling types will benefit the system as a whole.

1. Vertical Scaling

According to a technique known as vertical scaling, the infrastructure that manages the services must be expanded in response to the volume of requests. The service's internal code or database storage methods do not need to change as a result of this strategy.

The addition of new hardware elements like the Central Processing Unit (CPU), Random Access Memory (RAM), disk, and computing power to the machines is typically the case when scaling up your machines using vertical scaling. Your hardware and software capacities both increase with vertical scaling. To run your requests and handle them better, for instance, you could invest in much better database management software.

Although vertical scaling is a preferred strategy by many businesses, it is still expensive and occasionally wastes resources due to unrealistic scaling expectations. Some system designers prefer horizontal scaling over this approach because it is frequently difficult to estimate the response you will receive for your service.

What Are the Drawbacks?

This strategy is popular among small and medium-sized businesses because it allows them to increase resources without having to change the code or services they are currently using. Due to the need to distribute the data across more resources, this method, however, can cause significantly more downtime than horizontal scaling.

2. Horizontal Scaling

Instead of enhancing the physical capabilities of the machines through horizontal scaling, new machines will be added. This makes it simple to distribute the requests that one machine might otherwise have to handle. When compared to vertical scaling, horizontal scaling is more effective because more resources can be added.

What Are the Drawbacks?

You also need to be aware of software advancements that enable horizontal scaling. We can scale effectively, for instance, by developing automation software and utilizing the AWS cloud.

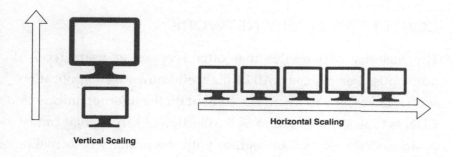

Vertical Scaling

Horizontal Scaling

Which Approach Should You Decide On?

In the end, the strategy you choose should be determined by the system you are developing. Going with vertical scaling makes sense when there are lots of small requests because the server only needs to handle more requests with harder tasks.

However, because more machines can handle even complex tasks that require a lot of retrieving and parsing, services that are dealing with complex tasks and are experiencing rapid user growth should think about horizontal scaling.

CONTENT DELIVERY NETWORK

The majority of websites that offer services to users receive numerous user requests. All of the well-known web application services use CDN to distribute content on the internet quickly. A CDN is typically referred to as a collection of servers that can be positioned across various regions with the primary objective of granting users faster access.

All of the media files will be easily sent to the user when a content delivery network is present within a service. To be precise, a CDN will typically speed up a website, which is great from a system design perspective to reduce latency and give users a seamless experience.

How Does a CDN Work?

To better explain how a CDN functions and how it can improve the end-user experience, let's use a straightforward example.

Sam is the creator of a brand-new video sharing website where users can upload videos and make them freely available for other users to stream. Sam has started utilizing a Dallas-based server to manage this application.

- Different Locations of the Users
- Dallas
- New York
- London
- Moscow
- Sydney

As a result, the Dallas server will receive a request whenever a user accesses a website. The service has users from all over the world, but the server is only present in one place, which is a problem. For users accessing the website from remote locations, this lengthens the response time.

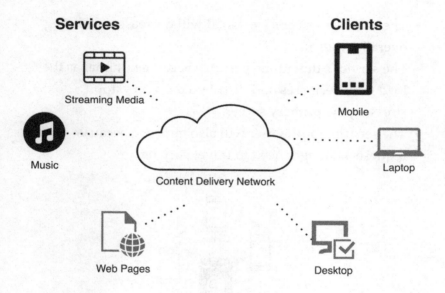

Services   **Clients**

Streaming Media

Music

Content Delivery Network

Mobile

Laptop

Web Pages   Desktop

For instance, a user accessing the website from Sydney will experience slower loading times than a user from New York. To be clear, the loading time will increase with distance from the server. In order to help the servers speed up for the users, CDN enters the picture at this point.

In essence, CDN shortens the path between the user and the server. In essence, CDN deploys a number of endpoints in numerous locations. Therefore, the CDN endpoint closest to the user's location will receive any requests made by users for the website before any other endpoints. The request will then be retrieved from the Dallas server by the CDN and sent back to the user. This process shortens the time it takes for a website to load.

Although a CDN has the direct benefit of increasing speed, there are also a number of potential indirect benefits.

- The primary server's workload will decrease, increasing overall retrieval.
- The service's downtime will also become minimal as the load time decreases and distributed servers stop stressing the primary server.
- The security for the user will also improve because requests no longer need to travel very far.

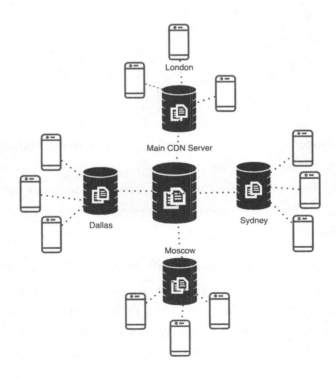

It is essential for you to use CDN implementation in various services because you are an expert in system design. In several case studies that we discuss throughout this book, CDNs will be brought up.

NETWORK LOAD BALANCER

It's not easy to run a website and scale it to accommodate millions of users. Your main responsibility as a system design expert is to increase the scalability of your systems while also giving users faster loading times.

What Happens?

As a result, whenever you create a service, the end-user typically accesses it using a device or web browser and submits a request to the internet. The request will be routed to one of the servers that runs the service from the internet. When there are very few users using the software applications, they typically operate in this way. The number of people using these services, however, grows over time, and as a result, businesses launch multiple application servers to handle the exponentially growing number of requests.

As a result, businesses will start scaling their application servers horizontally to include as many servers as they want in response to demand, rather than using a single application server. Multiple servers are now present, and the applications must once more figure out how to control them and send the requests that are being received logically. By system design experts during the internet boom that occurred twenty years ago, this is where the idea of load balancing was created.

A load balancer is either a hardware or, in some cases, a software device. The primary duty of the load balancer is to intercept all user requests and determine which app servers should receive them; additionally, a load balancer is able to gather data from these servers. Depending on the load being experienced, it has the ability to communicate and choose whether to turn off or restart the servers.

Businesses with millions of customers sending requests every second from various locations around the world are forced to use load balancing due to this dynamic auto-scaling advantage.

As we now know that load balancers have the ability to inter-cept traffic and distribute it to various app servers, let's examine how they actually carry out this capability.

Types of Load Balancers

1. Dumb Load Balancers

Assume there is a load balancer named "A," three app servers named "X," "Y," and "Z," and a load balancer. To distribute the requests to app servers, a dumb load balancer typically employs the Round-robin algorithm.

It will send the request to X, Y, and Z in that order. If more requests start to come in, they will be processed once more in the same order. It simply entails making successive requests to the accessible app servers. It is a better choice for companies with less than moderate traffic even though it is not a great solution.

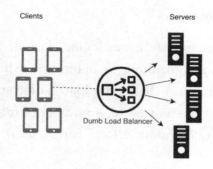

2. Smart Load Balancers

An smart load balancer will actually comprehend and take in data from the app servers. The load balancer will keep an eye on the app servers and stop sending requests to the server if an app server, like "X," sends a request that it cannot process any more data.

It costs more, but it makes more sense. Services that receive millions of requests daily from users typically use smart load balancers.

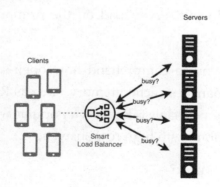

3. Hybrid Load Balancers

Hybrid load balancers are a particular class of load balancers that use particular algorithms to determine which app server should receive a request. To let the load balancer choose which app server to send the request to, a number of machine learning algorithms, such as "Random Select," can be used.

CACHING

Caching is a method that is employed by all devices to enable them to access content they require directly from Random Access Memory (RAM) rather than a database. Web applications use a variety of caching techniques.

For illustration, suppose you went to the Amazon website and retrieved the cat toy information for the first time. When you return to the same page later, it will load more quickly because the website has already retrieved the information and cached it on your browser or at the location where your specific server is located in the Amazon database. Because it improves user experience while reducing server load on the primary app servers, caching is effective.

It is crucial for you to comprehend how open-source software that efficiently manages cache memory, such as Redis, functions as a system design specialist. Redis is a popular web server used to build applications with high responsiveness.

How Does Redis Work?

Therefore, assume User "A" has asked the web application to retrieve a report from the database. The request will typically go to an app server first, then to a database. The request will change into a response and be sent to the user as a report once the database has been able to retrieve the requested information. This procedure could take anywhere from 20 to 40 seconds due to the time required to retrieve data from relational databases. Waiting more than 30 seconds to retrieve a straightforward report is unfavorable in today's world.

With cache memory, the procedure will vary, as illustrated below:

- A web server will receive the user's request first, after which it will be forwarded to a Redis cache server.
- The Redis cache server will respond to the user with the requested information in a matter of seconds if the user has requested any data. This action is referred to as a "Cache hit."
- The server will send a request to the database if there is no data, and once the data is retrieved, it will be sent to the Redis cache server to be saved. The report will be delivered back to the user once the data has been saved to the Redis cache server. This action is referred to as a "Cache miss."
- In order to monitor the database and add any new data that is added, the Redis server will also install a new service called "Cache worker."

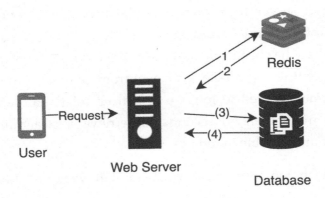

DATABASE TYPES

Information is kept in databases for later retrieval by servers using queries. When computers were first invented, computer programmers used databases that used microprocessors to manually store the data. Data retrieval becomes challenging because of this difficult work. However, everything changed in the 1970s as the idea of relational databases developed. After many years, we are now dealing with extremely powerful distributed systems that can quickly handle thousands of query requests. Knowing the various types of databases can help you better understand the challenges you'll face when developing intricate system designs for various services:

1. Relational Databases

All of the data will be stored in rows and columns in relational databases. A common query language for obtaining data from these databases is structured query language (SQL). Businesses all over the world still favor relational databases because they are stable and reliable. The only issue with relational databases is that the data must be structured; as a result, it is challenging to use a relational database when working with an unstructured service.

In this book, we have used Microsoft SQL Server, a well-liked relational database system, for our system design case studies.

2. NoSQL Databases

These databases follow a completely different philosophy than relational databases. Because the data in NoSQL databases is frequently unstructured, developers can alter the data as they go.

An outstanding example of a NoSQL database is Apache Cassandra.

3. Cloud Databases

The primary goal of cloud databases is to expand business hardware infrastructure. It is simple to scale or raise your scalability limit when using a cloud database. When compared to hardware infrastructure, these cloud databases are also simple to maintain.

The best example of a cloud database is Microsoft Azure.

4. Columnar Databases

In these particular databases, all the data is stored in columns rather than rows and columns. Analytical queries have more power with columnar databases.

A columnar database is exemplified by HBase.

5. Key-Value Databases

All of the data will be kept in this type of database using key-value pairs. Key-value databases can be processed quickly and are highly scalable. This kind of database helps e-commerce programs and multiplayer online games perform better.

A great example of a key-value database is Amazon DynamoDB.

What Is a Distributed Database?

The databases covered above meet various needs for various use cases. On the other hand, distributed databases and systems divide the data and store them on various servers. The main goals of distributed databases are to improve scalability and the user experience. From the standpoint of system design, any highly valued service ought to utilize distributed technology. If not, there will be more application downtime, which will result in revenue loss.

STATEFUL VERSUS STATELESS SYSTEMS

Distributed systems are used by all services to manage and handle client requests. Stateless and stateful architecture is regarded as the most crucial method for resolving the issues that distributed systems encounter in the field of software engineering. When designing a system or attempting to scale it based on the load your servers are under, a system designer must be aware of these architectures.

A system designer must first understand stateless and stateful systems in order to choose an architecture for a service based on how that service functions and determine whether a state is required for that service.

1. Stateless System Architecture

When the app servers do not need to store the state or context of the request made on behalf of the user, services use a stateless system architecture.

Say, for instance, that you created an online calculator and want to give the user the results. You have set up ten app servers to manage your service. Your request can be sent to any of the ten available servers because the calculation is the same no matter which user sends it. Stateless systems are those that do not store any state, context, or data.

2. Stateful System Architecture

When the app servers need to retain the context or data from a previous request in order for the response to be pertinent, a stateful system architecture is typically used.

Let's say, for instance, that our service is a chatbot that offers users popular places to visit nearby:

- User "A" logs in to the chatbot and asks for help in finding nearby locations based on their current location.
- After receiving the request, the app server will send the user a list of restaurants they can visit.
- The request should now be sent to the same server that handled the user's previous request when they choose a request to send again. If not, the answer won't be pertinent.
- To process requests quickly, stateful systems keep track

of the current context and previous conversations in the server's RAM.

MESSAGE QUEUES

Every server request to the database is typically synchronous. The server will respond to a request and carry out the request. Depending on how the process goes, the server will inform the user whether or not the request has been fulfilled when the task is finished.

Asynchronous requests are terrible for systems with many requests, even though they are excellent for small-scale systems. When our system databases are distributed, using asynchronous requests makes sense.

A messaging queue is typically used to process an asynchronous request. Every time a pool of requests is sent, an asynchronous request adds them to a messaging queue, where they are then processed sequentially by the application server.

APPROACH TO SYSTEM DESIGN INTERVIEWS

There are three main reasons why system design interviews are challenging to succeed in:

- Since most of the interviewers' questions are open-ended and may have multiple solutions, it can be challenging to put them into practice in the way they were intended.
- Poor performance can result from insufficient experience

in the field because system design is more of a
practically oriented subject.
- Lack of preparation

System design interviews can be aced with pure willpower and some practice, just like any other coding interview. The interviewer will primarily pay attention to the candidate's fundamentals, but they may occasionally push the boundaries to assess how many difficult tasks the candidate can handle.

We have provided numerous real-world solutions in this book that all follow a similar pattern, so we strongly advise you to approach any system design interviews using the strategy described below.

Clarify the Requirements

Asking questions and confirming the prerequisites for tackling a specific problem are crucial for candidates. A system may not be designed to meet the needs of the interviewer if you only have a general idea of what they want. Additionally, since each system design interview will only take an hour to complete, starting from scratch or working on optional components is not practical.

Clear communication with the interviewer is essential because it demonstrates your willingness to work with them and provide what they need rather than simply offering a system design theory that can't be scaled for their needs.

Define APIs

Most of the time, you must include the Application Programming Interface (API) parameters in the following step in order to receive user requests. In most cases, APIs handle HTTP requests and send responses either in HTTP or using JavaScript Object Notation (JSON).

For instance, the following is an API call for tweeting:

post tweet(USERID, Tweet, location, timestamp)

Estimations

The system design expert must estimate specifics for the system they are designing in this step. This step typically requires estimating the number of active users and determining an approximation of the resources required for better service maintenance.

Data Model

The system design expert will describe the database schema they advise for the service in this step. This section will also explain data partitioning and how the data will be retrieved from the databases.

High-Level System Design

The candidate should list all the components that will be used to develop a complex system design for the service in this section after the basic components have been covered. There will be a definition of every component, including the load balancer, file management systems, databases, and application servers.

Additionally, the candidate will outline how requests will be submitted and handled during peak periods. Before suggesting their suggested approach to scale the service, the system design expert should also take into account a number of alternative approaches. This will make it clear to the interviewer that the system design expert is knowledgeable about the advantages and disadvantages of each strategy.

Bottleneck Situations and Advanced Features

You can offer some solutions to deal with bottleneck situations that may arise due to peak request volumes once the system design is finished in the final section. The following issues need to be raised:

- Replication
- System downtime due to a single point of failure
- Monitoring services that will report system failures and provide updates
- Additional features that may be included in the future, but are not of importance right now

Now that you are aware of the fundamental ideas needed to become an expert in system design, it is time to look at the case studies we have provided. Check out these sample interviews to get a better idea of how a system design interview candidate should behave in order to get hired.

CHAPTER 2
PARKING LOT SYSTEM DESIGN

I n this chapter, we will begin by talking about a fundamental concept. This chapter focuses on applying the concepts covered in the previous chapter to develop a simple parking lot reservation and payment system. This is a typical interview question for businesses like Google, Amazon, and Apple. It makes it easier for interviewers to evaluate a candidate's aptitude for creating scalable systems, which is why many of them favor it.

You must first conduct a quick reconnaissance of the system in order to analyze any scalability-related issues that may arise. Although you may not need to write these questions down in front of the interviewer, you can quickly review them in your head for a more effective solution:

- What do parking lots do? What is the main objective of it?
- Who are the people who use parking lots?

- How will these users make use of this specific service?
- How much data must we be able to process?
- How many requests should we anticipate receiving?

Before moving on to the following section, take a piece of paper and write down a few of the answers yourself.

This straightforward system design interview is frequently used in the preliminary rounds to assess your knowledge of system design and object-oriented design. Be familiar with the concepts of classes, objects, and methods before reading this chapter. Class diagrams won't be covered in every chapter. However, it will be a good addition to this chapter to show you how an object-oriented design can be used to implement a system design.

UNDERSTAND THE PROBLEM

You'll be able to gauge the complexity of the system design by answering the first set of clarification questions. You can ask the interviewer the following clarification questions.

Candidate: I am fully aware of the principles of system design that should be applied when creating a parking lot service for customers. I can, however, design a system more effectively overall if I'm aware of your needs.

Interviewer: I'm glad you inquired about clarification. To create a system design for a parking lot service application that will be used by users who are willing to park in one of our parking lots, we need your assistance.

Candidate: So what do the functional specifications for this system design look like?

Interviewer: We require multiple entry and exit points for our parking lot service. In addition to storing the vehicle's information, creating a ticket, and generating the payment fees while exiting, we need to assign parking lot spaces according to the vehicle.

Candidate: What are the non-functional requirements?

Interviewer: Since it is impossible to lose parking data, the system must be dependable. The design should be highly available and consistent, and the system should manage ticket data information for at least five years.

Candidate: Many thanks. This knowledge will enable me to develop a complex system design for this use case. Just give me a few minutes so I can list class hierarchies and the system design I think will work best for this issue.

DATA AND SCALE ESTIMATION

Let's imagine that every day, 1,000 people actively try to park their cars in a parking space.

We will have 2,000 active connections per day with our server if a user communicates with the servers at least twice per day. This bare minimum of connections can be handled by one server with low latency, and bandwidth below 1MB/sec will also work for this system model.

We require at least a 10GB database that can store all the ticket information and details about every parking space that users are permitted to use for a year in order to manage the collected data. Therefore, it is advised to have at least a 100GB database with MySQL support in order to maintain a record for 10 years.

DESIGNING A CLASS HIERARCHY

We can design a system by constructing a class hierarchy because this is a straightforward system design problem. The software's class hierarchy will help us comprehend the different parts of the program and how we can use them to meet our needs.

Vehicle Class

In a parking lot, various car types are typically parked in the available spaces. There are many different types of vehicles, but for the time being, we will only support four of them: the motor-cycle, car, truck, and bus.

The size of the vehicles is used to categorize them here.

For instance, a van can be parked in a car spot alongside truck and bus spots, and a bicycle can fit in a motorcycle spot. Usually, we'll group cars according to their size:

1. motorcycle - small
2. car - medium
3. truck - large
4. bus - extra large

For better handling of our services, this vehicle class should also have the additional parameters listed below.

- license number: String

This will enable us to locate the vehicle quickly, or users to locate their parking space by using their license number as a search parameter.

- color: enum

Color can be used to distinguish a car from other, similar models in a parking space. This doesn't directly affect our service, but it might make it possible for employees to retrieve cars more quickly.

- type : VehicleType

As previously stated, this attribute will store the type of vehicle in the four categories of small, medium, large, and extra large based on size.

ParkingLot Class

A separate ID will typically be given for a parking lot because, like vehicles, there will be many parking lots in the area. Every time a parking ticket is created, the Parking ID is used to make sure the Ticket Number is unique.

- parkinglotID: int

Every time a car is parked, this class will be used for two functions, and the parking lot ID will be used to generate the ticket.

// This is a function that generates the Ticket entry

parking ticket entry (vehicle type)

// This is a function that generates the price for the Parking

Float exit (ticketID) ;

Here, the Ticket ID needs to be unique.

Ticket Class

When a vehicle is assigned to a parking space, a ticket will be produced using the following attributes:

- ticketID
- spotID
- license
- entryTime
- exitTime

The fare will be determined by entry and exit times. For automatic calculations, you can provide your fare service information.

ParkingSpot Class

The generated ticket will have a ParkingLotID associated with it. If a vehicle is present, this ID will be assigned and marked as "Occupied." If not, the ID will become a flag with the word "Available" on it.

- state - The state determines whether or not the space is reserved.

MAIN SYSTEM DESIGN

For the parking lot to become a truly in-demand service, our primary system design should concentrate on two issues:

- To check for available parking spaces and assign a parking spot in accordance with the type of vehicle, we must work on a sophisticated system design for vehicle entry.

- For the car to leave the parking space and generate a bill for the driver, we need to work on a complicated system design. Eventually, the vacant parking space should need to become available as well.

Vehicle Entry System Design

The service opens a request to check any allocation services when a user pulls into a parking lot to park their car. Let's call the service "Request Service," which will obtain the information from the vehicle class and send it to "Spot Allocation Service," which will use an algorithm to determine whether there are any open spaces for this specific vehicle type.

The status of the parking lot space will change from "Available" to "Occupied" if a spot is available, at which point the vehicle will be assigned to it. Immediately following the allocation, a ticket will be generated for our database and sent to the user. This generated ticket needs to include details like the vehicle's license plate number, ID, vehicle spot, and parking lot ID.

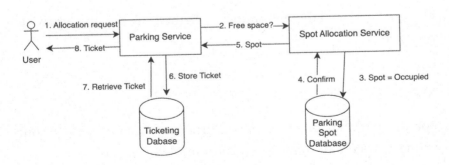

How Are Parking Spaces Assigned?

We stated that the "Spot Allocation Service" will oversee the vehicle allocation process in our vehicle entry system design. It is difficult to conceptualize this service, so we will talk about it using an example.

Stacks will be used to manage all vehicle allocation and parking lot services. Stacks are a useful data structure that can enable quick information retrieval for purposes such as determining whether parking lot spaces are available or not. Any additional data structures could lengthen the service user's wait time.

It is crucial to develop a plan to distribute parking spaces according to the type of vehicle, as we use stocks to assign spaces.

Example

Let's say a car owner chooses to utilize our service for parking lots. Our allocation service will first receive all the necessary information about the vehicle when the driver tries to check-in. The parking lot space availability for the type "Medium" will be checked once the service has determined that the car is a car and that it falls under the "Medium" category. If there are open spaces, everything will be fine, and a ticket will be generated. The space's status will immediately change from "Available" to "Occupied."

But what if there are no spaces of the "Medium" type available? Should we notify customers when there are no parking spots available in the lot? No. The service ought to be able to check the availability of additional parking spaces for various car types.

When looking for parking spaces for other vehicle types, a stack will be created; anything other than the current vehicle type will not be added to the stack. For instance, in this situation, the space designated for motorcycles is too small to accommodate a car. On the other hand, a car can be parked in an extra-large or large space that is typically reserved for buses and trucks.

Setting up Stacks

Instead of keeping the information about parking spots in a single stack, we should use multiple stacks to speed up the service's response time. It takes a while to locate the ideal location for the vehicle and fill it with people when there is only one stack.

The best strategy would be to create stacks based on size and list out any data structures pertaining to the number of available empty parking spaces for the service.

The list of vehicles that will be looked for varies depending on the stacks:

1. motorcycle - small, medium, large, and extra large
2. car - medium, large, and extra large
3. truck - large and extra large
4. bus - extra large

The service should inform the customer that there are no available parking spaces if there aren't any empty spots. We can also add a queue data structure to this system to increase complexity and give the user a waiting list number. Using the front-end user interface, they are always free to leave the line (UI).

From a database perspective, we must make sure that the database supports quick lookups because it must query numerous stacks to distribute parking spaces. Hash maps are recommended for this method because they can be quickly looked up using a key. MySQL has the additional capability of storing all hash maps, making it practical to implement.

What Happens During Parking Space Allocation?

The hash map key of a parking space will change from "Available" to "Occupied" whenever a new car is parked there, with the ticketID generated as a key. Therefore, the system will look up the spot whenever the user wants to remove a vehicle from the spot using the ticketID that is connected to the hash map. We can ensure that the driver can back out of the spot because it will immediately return the ParkingSpotID.

The hash map will be changed from "Occupied" to "Available" once the vehicle has been removed, and the ticketID will be saved to an external database for future use or stored in Redis to improve the experience for repeat customers.

Vehicle Exit System Design

We must first know the specifics of the user's vehicle and the parking space it is occupying before allowing them to leave the parking lot. The "Parking Service," which can employ a sophisticated algorithm to obtain all the information using ticketID, allows us to quickly retrieve this data. It will search the "Ticketing Database" using hash maps to find the value of the ticketID. We can quickly determine the ParkingLotID and the vehicle that is present there, as well as information like the license plate number, make, and model of the vehicle, when the 'ticketID' is found in one of these hash map values.

The parking service will send a request for a new service called "Deallocation Service" after it has verified that the vehicle should be removed from the parking space and the hash map value for the space changed from "Occupied" to "Available."

The system will automatically check the start and end times after the vehicle has been realigned in order to calculate parking fees for the user. To determine the fare based on the type of vehicle and the number of hours it has been there, use the separate service known as "Pricing Service." The user must then make a payment using one of our accepted payment processors.

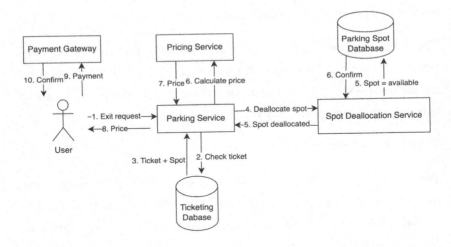

CHAPTER 3
INSTAGRAM SYSTEM DESIGN

D ue to their capacity to link their users with like-minded individuals, photo-sharing services like Instagram attract a lot of public attention. Some of the photo-sharing websites that have become well-known on the internet in recent years include Instagram, Flickr, and Picasa. With a little variation, websites like Pinterest can use the same system design as photo-sharing services.

To better understand the chapter and its approach, it can be a great idea to do some background research on the service before beginning:

- What is Instagram?
- What services are comparable?
- Does the app allow users to upload their own photos?
- How much information should we manage annually?
- What are the extra features that we might need?

Before continuing, take a pen and paper and independently respond to the following questions.

In this chapter, we'll create a stripped-down version of Instagram that lets users upload photos and follow other users. Each user's news feed will feature all of the most popular images from the people they follow.

UNDERSTANDING REQUIREMENTS

It's critical for candidates to comprehend the fundamental expectations of the interviewer in any system design interview. It is always advised to ask as many clarifying questions as you can because systems frequently become complex as scale increases.

Here are some clarifying inquiries you might make during an interview for an Instagram system design.

Candidate: If this design is very similar to Instagram, users can upload, view, and use photos on a service. Correct?

Interviewer: Yes. That is totally correct. The two applications are quite comparable.

Candidate: Should users be able to search for images and videos based on their titles?

Interviewer: Yes. They should be able to handle these tasks.

Candidate: Are users able to follow one another?

Interviewer: Yes. They ought to be capable. Normally, the photos in the news feed should be based on the people the user is following.

Candidate: Does the service need to be very available? What should the system's acceptable latency be?

Interviewer: Yes. The system ought to have high availability. For the generation of the news feed, a 200ms acceptable latency is preferable.

Candidate: Wonderful. What about consistency and reliability?

Interviewer: Consistency might suffer in this case. In other words, it might not be a problem if the user can't immediately access the photo that one of the followers uploaded. But reliability is a crucial factor. Never let any of the uploaded images or videos disappear.

Candidate: What about additional requirements like commenting, tagging, and photo searching?

Interviewer: Possibly down the road. We are currently looking for a simple system design.

You must look at various design considerations based on the interviewer's questions and responses. Use at least five minutes of the interview to match a complex design to the requirements.

DESIGN CONSIDERATIONS FOR INSTAGRAM

The design should be read-heavy and able to retrieve photos quickly based on the specifications given:

- Since users of the service are free to upload as many photos as they want, effective memory management was a requirement when developing the system.

- When using a mobile or web app to view the photos, there should be little latency.
- All of the data should be accurate, and data loss should never occur.

CALCULATING ESTIMATIONS AND CONSTRAINTS

Assume there are 200 million users overall and 10 million are active each day.

Nearly ten photos will be added to the app every second if one million photos per day are uploaded.

If we assume that each image has an average file size of 300 KB, the total amount of storage space needed for one day's worth of photos is

$1M * 300 KB*. — > 300 GB$

The total size needed to maintain the application with high reliability for five years is

$300 GB * 365 *5 = Approximately 550 TB$

DATABASE SCHEMA

Data partitioning must be understood thoroughly in order for an application to run as quickly as possible. A database schema will make the system designer aware of the data flow that takes place.

In this system, we need to store information about users, their uploaded content, and the users they are following. On this information, a user's news feed typically depends.

Photo Table

All of the metadata pertaining to a photo can be stored in the photo table. We need to create an index for the (PhotoID, Date-Creation) schema because it is necessary to fetch the most recent photos first:

- PhotoPath will help us in saving the data in a secure location.
- PhotoLatitude and PhotoLongitude will help us pick the location where the photo was taken.
- UserLatitude and UserLatitude will allow us to determine the user's location at the time of photo upload.
- DateCreation will enable us to determine the precise timestamp of the photograph's capture.

User Table

We can store the database schema unique to a user using the user table:

- Name: user account name.
- Email: email address of the user.
- DateOfBirth: birthday, and can help us recommend relevant data. On the basis of this schematic information, for instance, sensitive information won't be displayed to children.
- CreationDate: when the account was created.
- LastLogin: last login details of the user.

UserFollow Table

We can track the user's followers with the help of this table and create their feed using this data. For instance:

- UserID1
- UserID2
- UserID3

HOW TO HANDLE THE SYSTEM

Using a database service like MySQL to handle all the requests is advised. It is preferable to stick with services that support a relational database management system because we will be creating joins with our database parameters most of the time (RDBMS).

Instagram relies on media resources, so using a distributed file system like Hadoop Distributed File System (HDFS) will improve performance.

We will use the key-value storage option when utilizing RDBMS services like NoSQL to quickly retrieve items. When we upload metadata data to our servers, PhotoID will act as the key, and all other metadata data will be used when conducting searches or attempting to gather pictures of people on the list. We can make use of services like Cassandra to make this parsing easier.

The key value data will be replicated continuously by services like Cassandra to spread out the load that the system might encounter during peak periods.

Replicas can keep our system's data current even if they are not being read as frequently as they typically are because all the data must be permanently stored.

UNDERSTANDING DATA ESTIMATIONS

It is logical to first estimate the amount of data required for a photo-sharing service and redistribute it among several servers because this approach forces us to use a lot of data that databases typically can't handle.

Storing Only User Data

Databases should be made available with the sole purpose of storing metadata-related data for the user. To store their fundamental data in the system, each user needs at least 100 bytes. Therefore, if we apply this estimation to our active customers, we may require anywhere between 30 and 40GB just for storing user metadata. For reliability, all data should be replicated at least three times, so we require close to 120GB just for user data.

Storing Photo IDs

Every day, a large number of photos will be uploaded by all of our active users. We require 300 bytes for each photo in order to store the metadata data associated with it.

Therefore, just to store data about photo IDs, we need at least 2 TB of data for all the active users.

Storing User Follows

Our system is largely dependent on other users uploading their photos. We must create a column to hold the UserIDs of all users they are following whenever we create a separate row for newly registered users. This data will make it simpler for the system to create a dynamic, frequently updated news feed for the users.

We estimate that just storing the UserIDs of the people a user is following will require at least 4TB of data.

HIGH-LEVEL SYSTEM DESIGN

Our system design should, at the highest level, primarily concentrate on two scenarios:

- Uploading photos
- Searching or viewing photos

An image hosting server manages all of the primary connections for both of these services. All of the pictures should be sent by the image hosting service to a multimedia-ready object storage server. The database server should receive all additional media-related metadata information.

We can use different servers for write and read requests to boost system performance. It makes sense to use more powerful servers that can handle a lot of read requests because our system is heavily read.

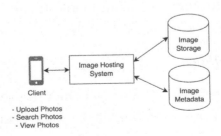

RELIABILITY AND REDUNDANCY

Due to the fact that we cannot risk losing data, our services must be extremely dependable. Therefore, it's crucial to keep multiple copies of each file on various servers to ensure that the data is accessible even in the event of a server failure. This makes sure that even if there is a problem with one copy, we can still access the data.

To various system services components, we must apply the same principles. We must ensure that there are replicas of all the services that can function normally in case any of them fail. Our data and services must be redundant in order for all of this to be possible.

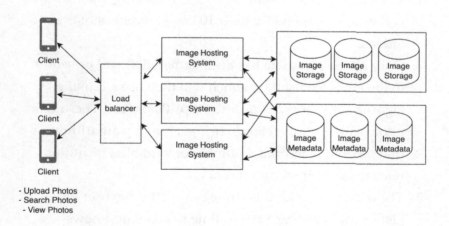

- Upload Photos
- Search Photos
- View Photos

NEWSFEED GENERATION

The method we take for creating a news feed is crucial for a service like Instagram because it is the news feed that keeps users hooked and returning to the app frequently for more. To make a dynamic news feed and make it appealing to the user, we must first create a list of photos that are popular with the people they are following. Popularity and relevance ought to be compatible. For instance, if a user consistently comments or likes User1's photos, User1 is more relevant and significant to the user.

How Can We Generate These Top Photos?

Assume that 100 photos must be produced by the service for the news feed. We can use ranking algorithms to show the user the best photos first rather than creating these photos at random.

The following steps should be followed by our news feed service:

1. Get a list of all the users the user is following, then gather the metadata for their 100 most recent photos or videos.
2. Once all the metadata has been gathered, it will be sent to the news feed server, which will then use a ranking algorithm to show the user the top 100 photos. These 100 photos are typically chosen using a ranking algorithm that takes into account a number of variables, including relevance, likeness, and recency.
3. The only issue with this strategy is that if the user has just begun scrolling, it takes time to generate a news feed quickly. In order to decrease latency, it is advised that the service pregenerate the news feed. If the user hasn't visited their news feed after a set period of time, you can also replace it with a different set of pictures.

PREGENERATING NEWSFEED

Pregenerating is a challenging process that requires a large number of servers to create news feeds for various users and store them in the server using the "Newsfeed" table. When a user opens the app, the service simply runs a query against the table to present the user with a list of the most popular results.

In order to avoid providing users with the same list twice, the service should also be able to check the timestamp that was previously generated. New content must be continuously added to the news feed.

How should we go about getting the news feed to the users after it has been generated?

Three strategies can be used to resolve this issue.

1. Pull

This method requires the client to ask the server to create a news feed and send it back to them. This is ineffective because a user cannot receive a news feed without making a request. Client requests frequently result in empty responses because there is no new data to include. This is inefficient and wastes a lot of resources.

2. Push

In a push model, as soon as the data is available, the server will push it to the user. The user must initiate an HTTP long poll connection with the server in order to receive updates for this to occur. However, because the server needs to push updates very quickly, this method can use a lot of resources for celebrities who have a large following or even for those who follow a lot of people.

3. Hybrid

The best of both worlds are provided by this method. All the accounts with a lot of followers can be switched to a pull model, and the accounts with few followers can be switched to a push model.

DATA SHARDING

The metadata sharding that we have gathered is crucial for handling our services efficiently. A list of photos based on the users the user follows or that are popular among the users they follow must be displayed when the user requests a news feed.

Data Sharding Based on UserID

We can therefore use the method to store all the photos associated with one user on one shard when the data is sharded. We are able to attach PhotoIDs to each shard for each image loaded to the service.

What Are the Issues?

- Hot users will receive more requests, making it harder to manage them.
- Because some users can use more storage than others, this is not uniform.
- What happens if there is not enough data storage while sharding and storing pictures? The data should then be automatically saved in a new shard by the system.

- It is also unreliable to save all user data and media in a single shard because if something happens to a shard and the data is lost, all user data will also be lost.

Data Sharding Based on PhotoID

The metadata should be sharded in this manner. In order to use this strategy, we must first figure out how to automatically create PhotoIDs as data is written. We can add auto-incrementing features to add new photos with a different PhotoID once the IDs have been generated. To reduce the load on the servers, we can install a load balancer or split the database into two, maintaining even and odd PhotoIDs.

How can we develop this system when the service popularity increases?

The amount of data you will need to shard will grow exponentially as you gain in popularity. We can create various logical partitions to efficiently store data using just one database. Additionally, we can create the location of these partitions using configuration (config) files and continuously update them whenever the database data changes.

You can use this information to more effectively generate a news feed once the metadata has been sharded. To quickly sort the most popular new photos from all the users an account follows, you can add a new value called creation time along with PhotoID. The creation timestamp can be automatically increased by using epoch configuration.

CACHE AND LOAD BALANCE

It is crucial to create a complex and effective content delivery network because we will be dealing with numerous users who are uploading thousands of photos every second. With the help of distributed servers, our CDN ought to be able to provide services worldwide.

Utilizing cache servers with metadata data that users are continuously pulling should be our main priority. This could result in higher latency and lessen the load on our data servers. Memcache can be used to deliver images that have already been read numerous times. To pull images that are already well-liked by users, use 80-20 caching rules.

CHAPTER 4
WHATSAPP SYSTEM DESIGN

This chapter focuses on answering system design-related interview questions about chat applications. Nowadays, almost everyone uses chat applications like WhatsApp, Telegram, and Facebook Messenger to communicate with friends, family, and coworkers. Different chat apps are created for various purposes. For instance, Slack is used by businesses and organizations to easily communicate with their employees, whereas WhatsApp is typically used to communicate with friends and family.

In this chapter, we'll use WhatsApp to demonstrate how a chat application's system design can become more complex as its user base grows.

Service Name: WhatsApp

Similar Services: Facebook Messenger, Signal, Slack

Difficulty Level: Medium

What Is WhatsApp?

WhatsApp is a messaging app that allows users all over the world to send text-based and multimedia messages. WhatsApp is primarily accessible through mobile applications. Additionally, WhatsApp offers a web interface that enables users to quickly send messages from the internet.

INITIAL REQUIREMENTS

Candidate: I already know how a chat system service like WhatsApp is designed, but it would be great if you could list out some requirements so that I can focus my approach and give you information in a thorough manner.

Interviewer: Sure. It resembles WhatsApp a lot. Supporting one-on-one conversations between users is our main goal. We should monitor each user's online and offline status in our chat service. For simpler data backup and retrieval, the entire chat history should be persistently stored.

Candidate: Would you please also list the non-functional requirements?

Interviewer: Sure. The user should experience very little latency from us, so the chat service must definitely be real-time. Our chat history should also be very consistent and reliable. Occasionally, availability may be reduced for better consistency.

Candidate: Do you have any additional requirements that I should be aware of?

Interviewer: Yes. Group chats are becoming more and more popular these days, so we also want to add this feature. Another feature that we are reluctant about is push notifications. I'm done now.

Candidate: I appreciate you being clear about your requirements with me. Please give me a few minutes to estimate various constraints before I give you a detailed system design for a service like WhatsApp that is similar.

CAPACITY ESTIMATION

Let's assume that our service has 100 million active users each day. Our system will still process close to five billion messages per day even if each user only sends 50 messages per day.

To store all messages for a day, even if they are 100 bytes each, we need at least 500GB of space. As there will be several multimedia messages that require more data resources, let's add a buffer of another 300GB.

*5 billion messages * 100 bytes — > 500 GB / day*

300 GB / day — — > Additional requirement for multimedia messages

All users' chat histories for a year must be stored in at least

*800 GB * 365 = 285 TB*

Keep in mind that in addition to chat information, we also need to store information like UserID and timestamp. Therefore, 300TB or more of storage space is needed to run the service smoothly.

We require a minimum bandwidth of 10MB/second if our chat service needs to handle 800GB of data per day. To determine the required bandwidth

800 GB / 86,400 sec = 9.2 MB/sec

HIGH-LEVEL SYSTEM DESIGN

We will have a chat server that serves as the focal point for all communications at the system level of our design. All users should be able to communicate with one another using this chat server. For instance, if A sends a message to B, the message from A should first be sent to the chat server that handles B's search before being forwarded to B by the chat server. Additionally, this chat server ought to be able to temporarily store the messages in the database.

Not all chat programs keep the information on their servers. For instance, WhatsApp stores data on your device. If the data is not backed up, it will all be lost. Conversely, messaging is stored in the cloud by chat services like Facebook Messenger.

To process a large number of transactions quickly, a chat server can be duplicated many times. But a real-time sync feature needs to be present on every server and database. If not, your service may experience an endless communication and message retrieval process.

The complete workflow is shown below:

1. User A will use their web or mobile application to message User B.
2. The message will first be received by the main chat server, which will then acknowledge it and notify User A.

3. The chat server will now send the message to User B and store the message A in the database.
4. Upon receiving the message, User B will notify the server by sending a received notification.
5. The server will then notify the first user, A, that User B has received the message after receiving confirmation.

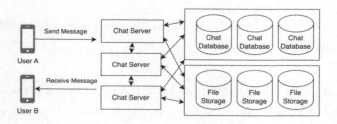

COMPONENT DESIGN

The server serves as a conduit between the sender and the receiver, which is relevant given the workflow described above. Our system server should be capable of handling the following at a high level:

- It ought to be able to deliver all of the outgoing messages and receive all incoming messages.
- Data management should be supported by the database.
- The server must keep track of the users' online or offline statuses and find a way to communicate this information to the appropriate users.

HANDLING MESSAGES

Two factors are of crucial relevance in the design of our system. It should be possible for the message sender to connect to the server and send the message. On the other hand, the receiver must be able to communicate with and receive messages from the server.

Regular messages can be sent to the receiver using either of these two methods:

- Pull model: The user must ping the server on a regular basis to see if there are any messages waiting for them. Because the server must constantly keep track of all messages received, store them in a separate data bucket, and send them all when the receiver connects to the server, the pull model is impractical, especially for a real-time chat service like WhatsApp. Due to the increased latency and the length of time required, the chat server will send an empty response if there are no messages. This is a very inefficient solution for us because it wastes a lot of resources.
- Push model: Typically, the user keeps a connection open to the server at all times. As soon as the device is connected to the internet, a connection to the server is established, and if there are any messages, the user is informed of them. Since the server does not have to keep track of messages in this method, the push model has no latency. Even so, there are still very little chances of latency on busy days, like New Year's Eve at 11:59 p.m.

HTTP Long Polling

We should be able to find a way to ensure that the clients are keeping an open connection with the server since we are currently satisfied with the push model. The push model can be implemented in our system design using either HTTP long polling or WebSockets. The client typically anticipates a response from the server right away after sending an HTTP request to it. However, when HTTP long polling takes place, the server might not have to respond right away.

For instance, the request will remain open rather than sending an empty response if the user sends a request and there are no messages for the user. When messages arrive, the established connection will send a reply right away, concluding the open request. The client machine will launch a new request for additional responses as soon as it receives the response. This strategy boosts the service's performance while also reducing latency.

So, we are now certain that our preferred method for using the push model to notify us of the messages we receive is HTTP long polling. But how exactly do we instruct the server to route messages to an active connection?

Hash Table

With the help of a hash table, the server is able to reroute the messages. A key and a value are typically present in the hash table. The UserID serves as the key in this instance, and an HTTP long polling object will serve as the value. As a result, whenever the server gets a message for a user, it immediately checks the hash table and connects to the available connection.

There are some adjustments we must be aware of when using this strategy. For instance, the server will attempt to connect to the open connection if a user sends a message to it. However, suppose the receiver isn't working. In this type of circumstance, the server must inform the sender that the recipient is unavailable, and we can either ask the server to resend the message or we can handle the situation by using a temporary storage technique without requiring the sender to repeat the entire process. Adding a code logic will save you from having to retype the message for the sender.

ESTIMATING CHAT SERVERS

Let's figure out how many chat servers we need to handle a large number of concurrent connections using the strategy we are confident in.

We require at least 10,000 servers that can support 100,000 concurrent connections if there are 100 million open connections at once. All of these servers must have UserIDs in order to make it simple to reroute requests to the server.

We require a load balancer before the chat servers in order to effectively manage all of these servers. As a result, whenever User A sends a message to User B, a software load balancer should be able to extract the UserID from the message and send it to the correct server that handles requests for that specific UserID. The server will then assume control and send it to the receiver.

Currently, millions of users' requests are being served by a load balancer and thousands of servers. We must provide more information about the server's delivery of message requests.

HANDLING DELIVER MESSAGE REQUESTS

The central server must complete the following tasks when a message is delivered:

- Store the message on the server.
- Send the message to the relevant person.
- Send a confirmation that the message was sent to the sender.

While the server is transferring messages between users, messages can be stored in the database in the background.

How Will the Messages Be Sequenced?

It's crucial for messages to be sent during real-time conversations in the same order as the conversation itself. The timestamp that is present for every message is typically used to order them in a message flow. The timestamp will typically reflect the moment the server received the user's message. Therefore, even if User A sent a message earlier than User B, but User B's message was received by the server first, User B's message will be sent to User A first.

How Will the Messages Be Stored and Retrieved?

We need to design our web servers so that they can handle small requests that are made in a large volume because all of our requests to the server will be for quick updates. A database must be used to store all of our messages. A user typically needs to send an asynchronous request to the user in order to store a message.

We should make use of an RDBMS service, such as MySQL, to ensure that all the small requests are properly handled. In addition to lowering latency, this will significantly lessen the load on all databases. We can solve the issue of fetching a large number of records by using services like HBase. Since HBase makes use of an HDFS, it is regarded as a robust, effective system for handling complicated operations.

HOW TO MANAGE USER STATUS

You may have noticed a status that indicates whether or not a user is online whenever you use a chat program. Several optimization principles can be applied to our system design to display a user status to other users:

- Design the service so that it connects to the server as soon as a user logs into the application to determine how many contacts are currently online.
- Every time they start a new chat, the user can send an HTTP request to see if anyone is online.
- The servers should be able to determine whether or not to display the online status after checking for a short while.
- In order to frequently check whether a user is online, users can also create a lengthy polling request. However,

because it wastes so many resources, this is viewed as being unnecessary.

DATA PARTITIONING FOR A CHAT APPLICATION

To store all of the user messages in the databases, all chat applications use and require a large amount of storage data. We have two main methods for partitioning.

Partitioning by MessageID

This method, which was once popular among message applications, is now viewed as impractical. With this method, the system will typically keep each message in a separate shard and pull them when the ID is called.

Partitioning by UserID

All messages and media sent by a user will be kept in a database shard using this partition. The userID value and a hash ID are typically assigned to each shard. The data should be encrypted so that other users cannot access it because it can only be retrieved by the user.

We need to create logical partitions and distribute the data in order to ensure that the data will remain trustworthy since we will typically be dealing with a theoretically infinite number of messages. It is also advised to use replication techniques to create copies of these messages for a predetermined period of time.

CACHE AND LOAD BALANCING

For messages, caching is less crucial because they won't be kept on a cache server for quicker retrieval. The same server that stores the messages should also host all of the cache that belongs to a user.

Since load balancers must continuously handle a large number of small requests, they must be as effective as possible. It is advised to use a system with an intelligent load balancer.

GROUP CHAT AND PUSH NOTIFICATIONS

These are the cutting-edge features that you can add to a chat application to increase its appeal to the intended user base.

Group Chat

In a database, each GroupChatID can be stored in its own row. Every time a group message is sent, the request is first sent to a load balancer. The load balancer then checks all the UserIDs in the group and sends the request to the servers handling the user messages. Additionally, we can use dedicated servers to only control group chats. Although every step is the same, group chats require more reading than one-on-one conversations do, so the server must be prepared to handle more reading requests.

Push Notifications

Services employ the method of push notifications to send messages to users right away even when they are offline. This will increase app usage, but the user may sometimes find it not useful. However, there are methods we can employ, like adding a favorite list to push notifications for crucial contacts. Push notifications are frequently more a part of the operating system design than the system design. To display these messages right away with a web app, you do need to access the push notification server.

CHAPTER 5
TWITTER SYSTEM DESIGN

Currently, one of the most well-liked social networking sites online is Twitter. Twitter users, in contrast to users of other social media platforms, rely on sending messages that are only 280 characters long. All logged-in users have the ability to tweet to their followers, who can reply to those tweets. Because of how it is designed, Twitter generates more content than any other social media platform, making it an addictive platform in its own right. As a system designer, candidates should concentrate on creating a complex architecture that is more accessible and frequently produces a dynamic timeline for Twitter users.

Similar to every other interview, make sure you have a sufficient understanding of Twitter's operation before getting ready to dive into the interview. These are some possible research-starting queries.

- What is Twitter?
- How is a timeline of tweets created on Twitter?
- What services are comparable to Twitter?
- What is the procedure for authentication?
- Are other types of media, like pictures and videos, permitted?

For a better understanding of the section below, take a piece of paper and jot down several ideas.

UNDERSTAND REQUIREMENTS

You should first clarify the various initial requirements with the interviewer for a complex architecture like Twitter. Giving the interviewer a long list of the tools that Twitter or other similar services use won't make a good impression on them. For the interviewer to evaluate your system design skills, you must first comprehend the problem, define it, and design a solution for it.

Candidate: What are the Twitter application's initial requirements?

Interviewer: Both posting and reading tweets must be possible for the user. Any of the tweets should be marked as a favorite. Users can follow Twitter users, and the timeline will be generated based on their list of followers.

Candidate: Can they only publish text-based tweets?

Interviewer: No, you can post pictures and videos as well.

Candidate: Therefore, I presume that a service like this needs to be very available.

Interviewer: Yes, the service must be very reliable and available. Never delete a user's previously posted tweets.

Candidate: What about latency and consistency?

Interviewer: For timeline generation, a 200ms latency is acceptable. Occasionally, consistency can suffer because of availability. If the user cannot view the tweet right away after one of their followers shares it, it is not a problem.

Candidate: Do you have any additional features in mind?

Interviewer: Tweet searches are a useful addition to this system design.

We can determine the capacity and identify restrictions based on the initial requirements that were mentioned.

CAPACITY ESTIMATION AND CONSTRAINTS

Assume that the platform has 10 million active users and 50 million total users. Assume that there are 20 million new tweets posted each day and that each user follows 100 people on average.

If each active user favorites ten tweets on average per day, we will have

*10M users * 10= 100M favorites*

We also need to have a reliable estimation of tweet impressions because Twitter users spend a large portion of their time reading other people's tweets. Our system will produce close to 800M tweet impressions per day if each user visits their profile three times and other people's pages five times, viewing ten tweets each time.

$10M(3 + 5) 10 --> 800M / day$

We must make sure that the text and media data uploaded in the form of tweets are stored without compression because reliability is extremely important.

For instance, 560 bytes are required to store each character in a 280 character tweet. At least 40 bytes are required for each piece of metadata, including the tweet ID, timestamp, and user ID.

$10M *(560 + 40) bytes -- > 6GB/day$

So, 6GB per day are required, even if each user only tweets once daily. We therefore require at least 60GB per day to simply store tweets, assuming that users tweet an average of ten times per day.

The close estimate is 6TB/day if a user uploads a media file for every fifth tweet.

The bandwidth will be close to 10GB/S for a better user experience because we are working with text and media tweets to create a timeline for the users. Any less will result in a poor user experience that will cause them to "rage-quit" the application.

UNDERSTANDING CORE FEATURES OF TWITTER

It is preferable if we can define the system APIs that will be used for the functionality of our service once we are aware of the requirements. Representational State Transfer (REST) APIs or

Simple Object Access Protocol (SOAP) APIs can be used to define APIs for our system.

Parameters

The default parameters that the APIs will use to enhance the functionality of our service are those that are listed below:

- parameterID: Every registered account will receive a parameterID. We can manage users who have been blocked or banned from the service with the aid of this ID. A user is typically only permitted to post a certain number of tweets each day. By using this parameter, users who go over their allotted quota will be throttled.
- tweet_inf -The tweet itself can be kept in this parameter. Typically, a tweet has 280 characters.
- location - This will use the user's current location or specifics from a location that was mentioned in the tweet.
- MediaID - This will be the default parameter for all the media files.

All of these parameters will be sent to the server in an API POST request. The tweet will be accessible via a generated URL. If not, there will be an HTTP error.

HIGH-LEVEL SYSTEM DESIGN

Our data requirements will be high because our system is read-intensive. As many as 300k requests to read and display data will be sent to the server each second.

A load balancer is required to route the client's request to one of the numerous application servers that are present in order to improve the consistency of the server. To reflect new tweets on users' timelines, all of these application servers require real-time update services.

What Happens?

- Anytime the client needs to retrieve tweets from their followers, they will send a request to the application server,
- The load balancer, which processes tens of thousands of requests each second, will receive the request first.
- To get the followers' tweets, the load balancer will send this request to an application server.
- A database will receive the request if it is to post a tweet. An effective file storage system will be used to store all of the media files.

Due to the traffic's nature, it is typically distributed unevenly. The application servers may need to handle more transactions, though, during busy periods.

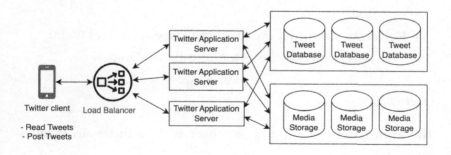

WHAT IS TWITTER DATABASE SCHEMA?

Any RDBMS service, like mySQL, can be used to store metadata and Tweet data.

The database schema will be divided into four tables.

Tweet Data

This database schema will focus mostly on information related to tweet metadata:

- TweetID - This entry will store information related to the Tweet. TweetID is unique for every Tweet.
- Content - This entry will be used to store data pertaining to the Tweet. Each Tweet has a distinct TweetID.
- Tweet lat - the Tweet's posting latitude and longitude coordinates. Users who are close to you will be pushed Tweets using the information you provide.
- Tweet long - The Tweet's posting location's longitude coordinates.
- Creation date - The creation time of the Tweet
- Favorites - The number of favorites the Tweet has received. This will frequently be automatically updated.
- Retweets - Information about the Tweet's retweet count. This will frequently be automatically updated.

User Data

The information pertaining to a user will be the main focus of this database schema.

- UserID - Information pertaining to the user will be kept in this entry. Every user has a different UserID.
- Name - This will save the username's information.
- Email - The default email address of the user will be saved in this. This can be beneficial when trying to recover an account.
- Date of Birth - Based on their age, these details may aid Twitter algorithms in hiding sensitive content.
- LastLogin - If users are gone for a long time, this information will enable servers to pregenerate timelines for them.

User Follow

All of the UserIDs for the accounts that the user is following will be stored in this database schema.

Favorite

All of the TweetIDs and UserIDs that the user has liked or retweeted will be stored in this database schema. Our algorithms will use this information to suggest relevant Tweets to the user.

DATA SHARDING

This heavy-read system necessitates that our system frequently manage numerous transactions. Multiple machines are needed because it is practically impractical to handle all of these transactions on a single server. The method used to efficiently handle all of these transactions with multiple systems is called data sharding.

We have several solutions for this issue.

Sharding Based on UserID

With this method, we can store on a single server all of a user's tweets and associated metadata. We can quickly connect a UserID to all of their data by using a hash function. As a result, whenever a query for tweets is made, the information is immediately parsed using the hash function and read.

However, there are some drawbacks to this strategy.

What if a user is well-liked and consequently receives a lot of requests, making it challenging for the server to handle these requests? Other users on the same server may also experience issues due to this load.

Additionally, this is not a consistent strategy because some users will use more data than others.

Sharding Based on TweetID

Every time a Tweet is written, a TweetID is assigned to it, and it is then stored on one of the numerous servers using a hash function at random. As a result, if a user searches for tweets, a request is sent to every server in the system to locate those tweets and return them to the user.

The method is as follows:

- The service will first learn the database structure of every user the account is following before making a request to find all of their most recent Tweets.
- The content will be sorted based on elements like

popularity and relevance when all the Tweets are sent back to the user using sorting algorithms.

- Although this can lessen the load on the servers because the service must query a large number of results, the latency will increase and the timeline will load more slowly as a result.

Sharding Based on Creation Time

This method makes it simple to order the Tweets according to their current popularity. It also requires a very small number of servers, but due to the fact that few of them will be in use and the majority will be idle, our server allocation will be terrible.

Each of the three strategies has advantages and disadvantages. With the aid of epoch, we can combine these three strategies for designing the Twitter system:

- For each Tweet that is entered into the system, a distinct TweetID should be generated. To make sorting for the system simple, a TweetID along with the timestamp should be present.
- The timestamp we employ must be auto-incremented and represented using epoch seconds. It will be simple for the system to find Tweets for a specific time when we increment this automatically.
- We can still evenly distribute the load across various systems by combining the epoch strategy with the TweetID or UserID sharing approach.

CACHE

There are a number of celebrities who use Twitter to share their opinions with the world because it is popular among a specific audience. It makes sense to use a caching mechanism for these well-liked tweets so that frequent requests and pulls are avoided. We can figure out how many servers we need to manage the caching process based on how frequently our users request the same tweets.

How Does the Cache Replacement Policy Work?

We don't need to keep track of dated trending tweets that users aren't currently reading very much. The least popular tweets in the cache server should be automatically deleted by our system, which should also replace them with a fresh, trending tweet.

Because our cache must be intelligent, we must develop algorithms that will check the read Tweet data automatically and identify the most popular ones. Typically, the Tweets on our cache server need to be those that 80% of users are reading.

Caching the Latest Data

Since Twitter is an updated service, many users frequently only see the most recent Tweets on their timeline. For instance, Tweets from the last three days typically account for 80% of those that users read. The number of "impressions" on a Tweet will decline over time.

In order to benefit from this circumstance, we can keep the Tweets from the previous three days in a different cache server. This server will handle every request. We can simply replicate the data across various servers because the cache server will be receiving a lot of requests. Replication will lighten the burden on the cache servers, making it simpler to retrieve the data.

We can use advanced linked lists to quickly add and remove the most recent Tweets from the cache server, enhancing its functionality.

TIMELINE GENERATION

We must ensure that the timeline generated for each user based on their following list is distinct for them and should be compelling enough because our system is heavily read. Real-time timelines are crucial, but we also need to make sure that there is little latency. Those with few followers typically don't encounter any issues, but if a user follows a large number of users on Twitter, things get challenging.

We must pregenerate the timeline and provide it to users upon request in order to ensure that our efficiency is high.

Offline Generation

Because the user can view their dynamic timeline when they log into their account, regardless of how many days they have been away from the service, offline generation helps to offer a special experience to the user. We should be able to continuously dedicate the user's timeline and keep it in memory so the user can view it more quickly.

However, a more recent timeline may eventually replace the one that was generated. To keep users engaged with the service, the user's most recent timeline should resemble their previous timeline quite a bit. Hash tables can be used to store both the UserID and the FeedID. Typically, a different FeedID will be used.

Typically, a feed will produce feed items. According to the users of the account who are following, every item in the feed will be different. Based on the user's activity, we should be able to generate Tweets. Users who follow more users, for instance, will see more than 1,000 items in their feed, whereas users who follow fewer users, on the other hand, will see less than 500 items.

We can always send requests to the backend servers to get more Tweets for the user if they finish their feed and want to query more Tweets from their followers.

What Else Can We Do?

We can monitor user login habits and tailor their news feed to the times they use the service most frequently.

Advanced cache mechanisms can also be used to automatically store the user's most popular and pertinent Tweets and display them as soon as the user scrolls through their timeline.

HOW TO PUBLISH TWEETS THAT ARE POSTED TO THE USER'S FOLLOWERS

Typically, Twitter users send Tweets to their followers. All users anticipate that their Tweets will be read. This is typically referred to as a fanout in popular culture. Everyone, not just famous people, anticipates that their followers will see their Tweets on their personal timelines. However, how can we actually push a user's Tweet to other users from the standpoint of system design?

Three specific models are available for use by services that are similar to Twitter.

1. Pull model - This model keeps all the feed information for fresh content in memory and sends Tweets to the server as soon as a request is made. The drawback of this model is that users won't receive new Tweets right away. It will also result in significant resource waste because the majority of the time, when a user submits a request, the response is empty.

2. Push model - A Tweet will be sent to all followers using a push model as soon as it is posted. This is interactive and gives Twitter users up-to-the-minute information. A user's feed will be generated along with the most recent Tweets if they are active. However, if a user is inactive, the relevance and popularity of the Tweet will determine whether or not it appears in the user's timeline. The user must always open a lengthy poll request with the server for it to function as intended. The push model, however, is not as practical for popular accounts because it requires pushing the request for a large number of users —sometimes millions—to be successful.

3. Hybrid model - This strategy strikes a balance between the benefits of both the push and pull models. With this model, users with fewer followers can use the pull model, while those with more followers can use the push model. This method will also conserve a significant amount of memory and bandwidth each day.

Keep in mind that when pushing data, you do not necessarily need to push data for users automatically, particularly if they are using mobile devices. Utilize methods like refresh to update the timeline. However, since network resources are not a factor in web browsers, the timeline can be updated automatically.

CHAPTER 6
YOUTUBE SYSTEM DESIGN

O ne of the most widely used services on the internet right now is video sharing. It takes a complex system design and a large amount of storage space to create a service like YouTube. You can use this chapter to formulate responses to system design questions that may require you to create websites like Netflix and Hulu. To help you comprehend a fundamental system design for this kind of service, we will use the free and well-known video sharing website YouTube in this chapter.

Like every time, a quick YouTube search can give you a good idea of what the interviewer might be looking for in the system design.

- What is YouTube?
- How are videos uploaded to YouTube by users?
- What are the steps for YouTube video uploading?
- How do the algorithms on YouTube suggest videos?

- How do the video recommendations on YouTube work?

Before beginning the interview portion of this chapter, take a piece of paper and independently generate various ideas.

UNDERSTANDING REQUIREMENTS

Because developing a complex system design is crucial for video streaming websites, you must first ask the interviewer some fundamental questions to determine the level at which you must develop a system design.

Candidate: I am aware of the system design used by popular streaming website YouTube. However, because of YouTube's much larger scope, I must get your confirmation of the requirements.

Interviewer: Sure. All we want to do is build a website that resembles YouTube. Users from all over the world will be able to sign up and upload videos to the platform. The ability for users to share, view, rate, and report videos is essential. We can also include the comments' functionality.

Candidate: Perfect. Should each video have a likes and dislikes counter?

Interviewer: Not necessarily for the time being, but having that feature would be acceptable.

Candidate: Should the user have access to sophisticated algorithms for searching?

Interviewer: Yes, the search must be efficient, and all results must be kept in a remote database so that users can be recommended videos.

Candidate: Great. The non-functional requirements, what about them?

Interviewer: The system must be extremely dependable in order for the uploaded videos to remain intact. This has top priority.

Candidate: What about availability?

Interviewer: The system must have high availability. It is acceptable if some users do not see the videos almost immediately after they are uploaded when consistency suffers occasionally. However, keep in mind that viewers should have a real-time experience. The users shouldn't experience any lag at all.

Candidate: What other cutting-edge features do you want to use?

Interviewer: In later versions of the service, we want to add a number of additional features like video recommendations, trending videos, channels, and subscriptions. They are currently outside of our scope. Just a simple system layout for online video services like YouTube will do.

Candidate: I'm grateful. Now that I have all the information I need, I can design a complicated system based on your specifications. Please give me a few minutes so I can run through the details with you.

CAPACITY ESTIMATION

Assume there are 1 billion users overall and 200 million of them use our service every day. If a user watches at least two videos per day, on average, the number of video views per second will almost be

200M * 2 / 86,400sec — > Close to 4k videos/sec

Let's assume that the read to write ratio is 200:1, which means that we have about 40 videos uploaded every second.

4k / 200 — > 40 videos / sec

What are the storage estimations?

Let's assume that every minute, 100 hours of videos are being added to our service. If managing this flow requires 100MB every minute, we might require at least 600GB every minute.

100 * 60 100 = 600 GB /min

As we will be using a number of compression and replication techniques to reduce the file size, the rate can drop to at least 500GB/min.

What are the bandwidth estimates?

According to the calculations above, our bandwidth will likely range from 3GB/second. Videos may lag as a result of a reduction in bandwidth. Since we have no other option, we at the very least require a bandwidth of 5 GB/sec to handle even during our service's busiest times.

ABOUT SYSTEM APIS

Either SOAP or REST APIs must be used when developing a service similar to YouTube.

To set our APIs apart from the competition, they must be effective and able to handle a large number of useful parameters.

Parameters for Video Upload

- APIkey - The account's developer key will be obtained in this way. The system will be able to access any information about the user's quota limits using this key. Sometimes, a user's developer API key should not work as intended if they are banned or shadowbanned from uploading any more videos.
- VideoTitle - The title of the video that the user is trying to upload or find will be collected by this parameter.
- VideoDescription - The video description, which is typically available for every video on the service, will be the subject of this parameter's information gathering. The text information provided here can be used by our search engine algorithms to provide results for videos.
- Tags - Any hashtags or other tags that the user uploads to increase their reach or make it easier to upload popular videos.
- CategoryID - We will be able to identify the video's category using this ID. Politics and history are two distinct categories, for instance. When uploading the video, the uploader chooses these categories to display their content to the appropriate audience.

- Language - The original language in which the video was uploaded
- Location - The geolocation information from which the video is uploaded will be included in this parameter. This will enable us to share this video locally.
- VideoContent - The actual video file

A successful HTTP request will be sent once all of these parameters have been sent to our servers and our video has been uploaded.

When a user uses our service to search for a query, our API parameters will change:

- UserID- This is the UserID for the logged-in user who is looking up a particular keyword. For this browsing session, we can create a random ID if the user is not registered.
- Query - The search term the user is looking for will be included in this.
- Location - This will save the user's latitude and longitude when they search for a query.
- Maximum - The number of videos that must be returned to the user is specified by this parameter.
- Page - The page number when searching for videos is represented by this parameter.

A JSON response containing all the videos matching the query will be sent once the request has been sent.

In order to stream video on your website, the following extra information must be sent to the service:

- APIkey - The UserID or DeveloperID of the person accessing the service will be sent in this way.
- Video - The video ID of the specific video you're attempting to stream
- Offset - The information about where the user must watch a video is stored in this parameter. When a user is viewing a video on two different devices, this offset is useful. Our video viewing history could be synced thanks to offsets.
- Codec - The codec that the video wishes to play in must be sent as a system parameter.
- Resolution - The resolution that the user has chosen will be sent along with this parameter.

The video will begin streaming from the specified offset as soon as a request is sent.

HIGH-LEVEL SYSTEM DESIGN

To gain user popularity, a service like YouTube needs to have a number of intricate components.

Client: The customer is one of our users who wants to upload a video or view one that another user has already uploaded.

Processing Queue: A processing queue will be used to automatically process and encode any video that is uploaded to our servers. The ability to create thumbnails for the video should be included in this processing queue.

Encoder: The encoder's function is to change a video's format after it has been uploaded. Depending on the output device you are using, the encoder will alter the resolution and stream the video using a variety of codecs.

Storage: We should store all of our videos, thumbnails, and metadata in a distributed file storage system that can handle large files.

User Database: The user's information, email addresses, and birthdate will all be stored in this database.

Metadata Service: All of the metadata that can be used to search or rank videos will be stored in this database. We may use metadata information such as likes, comments, and views in this database service.

DATABASE SCHEMA

A DBMS service, like a SQL database, should be used to manage all the data. This metadata data can make it simple for programmers to create algorithms that can search videos or give reliable user recommendations.

Video Database Schema

- VideoID: unique identifier for every video
- Title
- LikeCount
- DislikeCount
- ViewCount
- Thumbnails
- OwnerID
- VideoSize
- Description

Video Comment Database Schema

- CommentID
- VideoID
- UserID of the commenter
- Comment
- Timestamp

User Database Schema

- Name
- Email
- MobilePhone
- LastLoginAt
- Gender
- Age

COMPONENT DESIGN

It is clear that the system is read-heavy by looking at the require-ments and the database schema. Every time a video is uploaded, there will at least be a 200-fold increase in views.

We must use distributed file management systems like HDFS to ensure that the media is stored effectively.

How to Read Traffic Efficiently

It makes sense to separate the read and write data conditions to different servers because there will be more read data. A config-uration should first contain all the metadata data, and once the write data operation is complete, any user query will result in a read data operation. However, because of this method, there will be a very slight latency of a few milliseconds when the video is first uploaded. This won't be an issue, though, as the video will be sent to the read servers for faster access moving forward.

How Will Thumbnails Be Generated and Stored?

Thumbnail generation is difficult because we need to use separate servers to store all the high-memory media that we want to store:

- To handle the thumbnails better, we should be able to compress them into low-quality images.
- As more thumbnails will be viewed by users without any of them being clicked, it is critical that we develop effective solutions that can handle the higher read rates.

We can use the Bigtable method to generate and read thumbnails effectively. As a result, we can use cache servers to quickly load popular thumbnails and regular servers to create additional thumbnails. A better user experience can result from having files in memory because it can lower latency.

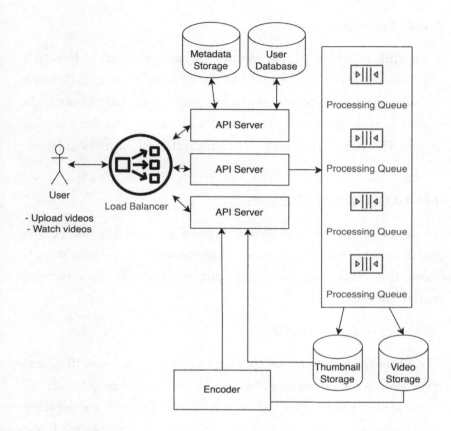

ADDITIONAL COMPONENTS

Video Uploading

The complicated process of uploading uses a lot of network bandwidth. The upload process may occasionally end abruptly due to the client's poor network connections. In order to automatically resume the video upload procedure without having to worry about starting it from scratch, our service must make use of caching.

. . .

Video Encoding

Our built-in video player should be able to play videos in a variety of formats on a variety of devices. Additionally, different browsers employ various encoding principles. The moment the video is uploaded to our servers, our video encoding should begin. The video shouldn't go live until the encoding is finished.

METADATA SHARDING

We need to use a distributed system to manage our service because it is read-intensive and consumes a lot of resources to store this data. We can share our multimedia data using a variety of methods.

Sharding Based on UserID

With this strategy, we can attempt to store all of a specific user's videos on a single server. This server will be contacted with any requests for the user or video. We will also utilize a hash function to store all of the user-related metadata on this server. Every time someone searches for a video or a user ID, the system looks for the keys from various servers and reads them. A hash function has a key. We can send a request to all the servers to find the suggested videos for the keyword rather than having users search for it directly.

All of these videos will be analyzed by a central server, which will then rank them according to a complex algorithm.

What are the issues?

- The main issue is that if a user gains popularity, the number of queries directed toward that server will increase, making it challenging to process requests from other users. This is not a workable answer.
- Because only a few users will use a lot of data, uniformity will also be an issue. From a data management standpoint, this is unfair.

We can replicate and redistribute the servers to address these two issues, but this is typically a difficult process.

SHARDING BASED ON VIDEOID

Every video that is uploaded using our service will receive a special VideoID, as was previously stated. Once the VideoID has been created, it will be transmitted along with all the metadata information to one of the numerous random servers that are available. Therefore, whenever a search query is made, the request will be sent to all the servers, and the service will return a set of videos based on the video metadata information. These videos can then be ranked according to how popular and relevant they are.

This method enables us to avoid overloading any one server. The most well-liked videos can also be cached for the system's benefit so that they can be listed more conveniently.

VIDEO DEDUPLICATION

It is crucial for the system design to have a strategy for preventing video duplication while maintaining video services like YouTube. Uploading a video or a portion of a video to the service with a different encoding and a minor change to the overlays is referred to as duplication of a video.

- Duplicating videos wastes memory and energy.
- Duplication of video reduces the cache memory's intelligence.
- The network bandwidth is increased by video duplication.

This will also have an immediate effect on the end-experience, user's and watching videos frequently experiences lag.

How to Stop Video Duplication?

At first, it takes a lot of resources to find duplicate videos. In order to identify videos that might be using duplicate content, we need to be able to use machine learning algorithms like phase correlation. Since no algorithm is flawless, occasionally we may detect videos that don't actually contain duplicate content. We should use inline deduplication, which checks the video for duplicates before uploading it to the servers, in order to conserve resources.

LOAD BALANCING AND CACHE

A load balancer should receive all requests before sending them to a video service because video services frequently receive thousands of requests per second. The request will then be routed by this load balancer to the relevant server based on the logical replica of the query.

While this is a good strategy, things could get complicated if a popular video received more requests, which would fill up a physical server. Consistent hashing is a solution to this issue. Consistent hashing automatically switches a request from a server that is busy to one that is less busy. As a result, there will be less load and fewer delays. HTTP redirection is quick and has no negative effects on performance. However, rerouting the request to a server that is closer to the user's location can reduce latency and offer a better latency overall.

We can apply the 80-20 rule to create a better caching system. Every day, any video that is 80 percent read will be stored on a cache server. The cache server should be dynamic and capable of deleting data from the server automatically if there is a decrease in hits.

CONTENT DELIVERY NETWORK

A distinctive CDN should be created for a video service that operates on a global scale and serves millions of users. This strategy will increase the end user's streaming capabilities while also saving bandwidth and memory. However, because we must distribute servers across several different regions, it is expensive.

- In order to increase the likelihood of a video loading more quickly, CDN can replicate content in various advantageous locations.
- Since CDN permits caching, the majority of the videos

will run directly from memory and consume less bandwidth.

However, only well-known videos should use CDN. We can simply distribute from various data centers around the world for all other videos that are less well-liked and have fewer views.

CHAPTER 7
TINDER SYSTEM DESIGN

The system design for dating apps like Tinder will be the main topic of this chapter. With the help of their service, Tinder has assisted thousands of couples in actually meeting one another, becoming a cultural phenomenon in the process. More than 50 million people around the world use the Android and iOS apps for Tinder, which is widely popular. For its business, Tinder doesn't have a web interface and is entirely reliant on mobile apps.

Perform thorough research on Tinder to comprehend what it is and how it works before the interview. Here are a few inquiries to get you going.

- What services are comparable to Tinder?
- How does Tinder's authentication process work?
- How does Tinder's recommendation engine operate?
- How engaged are the users?
- Are the swipes accurate?

- How effective is the matching?

UNDERSTANDING REQUIREMENTS

It's crucial to probe during any system design interview to learn the fundamentals of what the interviewer is looking for from you. These inquiries will assist you in keeping your attention on the client's priorities without straying from their demands. Additionally, this process will aid interviewers in comprehending your level of subject-matter technical proficiency.

Candidate: So, as we all know, Tinder is a dating app. What do you assume from the authentication procedure?

Interviewer: The user must be able to sign in to the application, such as Facebook, using OAuth. We'll make an effort to use as many different authentication techniques as we can.

Candidate: The user typically swipes accounts to the left or right, so when two users swipe to the right, it must be a match, right?

Interviewer: Yes, that is basically how the application should function.

Candidate: Both users should be able to communicate with one another after a match is made.

Interviewer: That's correct.

Candidate: Exist any features that would help us monetize our app, such as super likes?

Interviewer: Yes. There should be.

Candidate: Can you describe the system's latency and real-time availability?

Interviewer: Low latency is required, but reliability sometimes comes at the expense of consistency.

Candidate: That gives me all the details I need to design a thorough system for Tinder. Please give me a moment to summarize my points.

Interviewer: Definitely.

HOW SHOULD TINDER WORK?

Now that you are familiar with the interviewer's requirements, it is critical to comprehend logically how the Tinder algorithm actually functions:

1. Active Usage

Between two people willing to start new relationships, Tinder serves as a bridge. Therefore, it makes no sense for the algorithm to link with users who aren't active on the app. As a result, linking two users who are active on the application requires consideration in our system design.

2. Collect Tags

Using the OAuth process, our algorithms must be able to gather enough data about the user. The algorithm must immediately extract the user's location, age, gender, and likes using the platform's API after they log into their account using a platform like Facebook. Users should be able to find better matches thanks to the Tinder bio and pictures uploaded to the website.

3. Group User Base

We must ensure that users are given a random score by the algorithm in order to be divided into groups because there will be a large number of users, and each will have different preferences. Based on their preferences and likes, this grouping will make it easier to match users.

4. Identifying Bad Actors

We need to make sure that excessive swiping is viewed negatively in order for this to be a reliable service. A bad indicator for linking people should also be considered when not swiping at all. In order to decide whether or not to include the user in the recommendations, the algorithm should be able to determine how frequently they message after a match.

5. Progressive Taxation

The last requirement must guarantee that more matches and swipes are distributed evenly among all users. Our algorithm must be aware of the fact that some accounts frequently garner more attention in order to avoid recommending them to too many users.

Here are a few more ideas to help our Tinder application system design stand out from the competition:

- Low latency is necessary in order for potential matches to load quickly.
- For better profile matching, the system design must be made so that it is simple to shard and distribute profiles.
- For better recommendations, a full-text search is required.

USING ELASTICSEARCH AND SHARDING THE DATA TO MAKE QUERIES FASTER

Developers can use Elasticsearch to produce quick search results. We must ensure that the data is geographically sharded in order to speed up Elasticsearch queries. Elasticsearch uses indexes to directly search the text, making it more dependable than standard text search.

Since most users will be looking for matches in their immediate area, our Tinder system design should ensure that the data collected is clustered for a specific location. The default 50KM setting on the Tinder app itself was available for customization.

We must make sure that there are servers available for particular locations in order to shard the data according to geographic location. For instance, a particular state in the US might have its own server for the data to be stored, so when launching the application, we need at least 100 different servers. Depending on how many queries are coming from a particular location, we can choose the servers that will serve that region.

We need to use metrics like unique user count, query count, and active user count so that we can decide performance for that area and which locations need more servers and how to distribute the load.

RECOMMENDING USERS FOR SWIPING

To make this work, the system design should first concentrate on segmenting the world map into several small areas, and then allocate servers based on the volume of requests coming from each area. In order to give the end user reliability, servers should be allocated based on the requests.

Since the servers are frequently dispersed, the system design should concentrate on matching the users who are present in the neighborhood, so the procedure for connecting the users needs to be carefully considered.

The Google S2 Library can help you use the client's location to send the requests to a specific server rather than sending them to a random server, which is how to technically make this possible. If there are multiple servers, the system will evaluate each server's latency before deciding where to send the request.

What happens?

Therefore, the application will begin sending the user's lat-long to the application component, where the server's locations are stored, whenever a user opens the application and waits for the recommendations to pop up. Now, the server will be selected based on the information provided, and based on the information provided by the user, a match will be found in that server. Users occasionally choose a location that is more than a few hundred kilometers away, and at this point, information about the user is sent to several servers in an effort to find a potential recommendation match.

TECHNICAL UNDERSTANDING

1. Users must first log in to the application using Facebook or another service of a similar nature, after which all

information provided is sent via an HTTP / WebSocket service to an Elasticsearch feeder.

2. Since reliability is crucial and should be persistent, a copy of the information obtained will be saved for safekeeping. For quicker Elasticsearch recommendations, the system also keeps a second copy.

3. The system's design suggests using a service like Kafka to manage Elasticsearch efficiently.

4. The lot-long information will be sent to a service that matches different servers to the user's application once the Elasticsearch service recognizes the user is looking for a recommendation. The Google S2 Library typically makes this mapping possible.

5. Once the server is located, the sharding process kicks in, and the user will see a variety of potential recommendations on their screen. These are typically produced with the help of the mobile HTTP / WebSocket service.

Once the suggestions have been shown, the user has the option to swipe left or right. Only when you swipe right does a match occur.

MATCHMAKING

After the suggestions are given, the Tinder app must concentrate specifically on a two-profile interaction basis. Since people frequently use dating apps similar to Tinder to meet people with shared interests, it is crucial that the system design proposal have a robust method to address this condition.

Let's take the case of two profiles, X and Y, as an example.

Different situations can be possible:

1. X and Y both make a right swipe because they are interested in one another.
2. X swipes to the right, but Y doesn't.
3. X and Y both swiped left because they had no interest in one another

More than a million matches take place every day, it is obvious when we create a program like Tinder. The number of matches will inevitably rise as the user base expands. We can use cells, or a group of cells, to handle a lot of recommendation queries and the swipes that are registered to these queries in order to ensure that our matchmaking service is as effective as possible. Typically, this process operates in conjunction with the previously mentioned geosharding process.

Let us give you a brief example in order to make it as easy as possible for you to comprehend this intricate system design.

A user who swipes at least 20 or 30 times daily receives at least 100 recommendations per day. We can use a set of cells to register a specific user's swipes instead of needing a separate matchmaking service for each swipe.

No data is saved in the matchmaking service when a user swipes left after being recommended, other than a record that the user is not interested in a specific user so that they won't be recommended in the future.

In contrast, if a right swipe is made, the matchmaking service will record the user's data and store it in Redis with a format like "X Y," which can then be used to determine whether or not the other user has also used a right swipe. If not, the users will not be able to match because this information will remain in Redis forever. However, if the user swipes to the right, the WebSocket activates and an animation announcing "It's a Match" is shown.

A copy of it is necessary to improve services for the user because as a service, you must ensure that all data sent into Redis is always accurate.

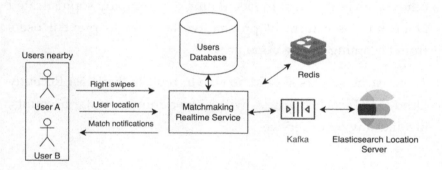

UNDERSTANDING CONTENT MODERATION

As a dating service, it is crucial to guarantee that all user-submitted content is moderated. Spam grows when the system doesn't moderate it enough, and user engagement suffers as a result. Because it uses thorough moderation techniques when designing its system, Tinder is well-liked.

Tools like Prometheus can help us provide features that make it simple to log various user events and automatically alert the systems if there is any spam or content that is prohibited by the privacy policy.

CACHE

Every account on a dating site is typically quite well-liked by other users. The load that they might place on our primary servers can be reduced by using a cache server. To store data about all the user-related information, you can use programs like Memcache. Keep in mind that just because an account is popular doesn't mean it should be recommended to a lot of other users in the area. In fact, dating apps employ sophisticated algorithms as a form of progressive taxation to prevent users from becoming overly popular.

These cache servers should be able to replace the Least Recently Used (LRU) cached entries with newer, more popular accounts, just like any other service.

COMPONENT DESIGN

To handle all the features that we have already discussed, our system design should have multiple dedicated services.

Images

Before discussing any service, it is crucial to understand that files should be used to store images because they take up less memory than large binary objects do. Files are less expensive, and with a sophisticated CDN, managing these media files is simple.

Database Schema for Images

- ProfileID
- ImageID
- FleURL

Using FileURL , you can also add image files from other social media platforms to the Tinder app.

Profile Service

- This service will take care of user information-related features.
- A user will be able to log in using suggested services.
- This service will be used to authenticate all user requests, which will then be sent to a gateway server once they have been approved.
- If the user is well-known, this service will be able to store images to a remote database server and a cache server.

Gateway Service

- Between user requests and the numerous other services that make up our service, this service serves as a mediator.
- Here, all requests will be checked and validated.
- Reduce the complexity and offer a straightforward API.
- Because the gateway service will be able to send requests to multiple services at once and receive responses from them almost immediately, the number of API pull requests will decrease.

Recommendation Service

This is what keeps our service running smoothly. To link two accounts that are similar to one another and may like one another, the entire database schema that we have so far stored and used for matchmaking will be chunked and partitioned:

- SQL or NoSQL databases are used
- Sharding, which primarily takes the form of horizontal partitioning, can occur to lessen the load on the servers.
- Both unidirectional and bidirectional query requests are possible. to refer others to one another
- The database will contain all of a user's swipes, and it will be used to determine how likely it is that they will connect with another user.

Message Service

Every time two users find one another, this service is started. Users of Tinder cannot communicate with one another until that time.

Connection Protocol

Users can communicate with one another using the message service once it is activated, just like in a standard chat model. Extensible Messaging and Presence Protocol (XMPP) or the client-server protocol can be used to send messages quickly from one user to another. This service is used by all other chat programs, including Facebook Messenger and WhatsApp, to enable user communication.

CHAPTER 8
UBER SYSTEM DESIGN

We'll talk about creating a sophisticated and reliable system design for the Uber backend in this chapter. One of the many services that facilitates rides with drivers who have cars for passengers is Uber. Compared to other system design mock interviews we have looked at before, it is quite complex. To better understand the topics we will be covering, we strongly advise you to use the mobile or web interface of Uber or other similar services before reading this chapter.

What Is Uber?

Uber is a service that facilitates connections between people looking for rides and people waiting to offer their services via an easy web or app interface. Typically, when a user uses their app to request a ride, an Uber driver is assigned to them and will pick them up and take them to their destination within a short period of time.

Due to backend technology, Uber now offers the ability to order food. As it is more complicated and helps the interviewer understand your technical expertise on the subject, we will focus on the ridesharing service system design for this example.

UNDERSTANDING REQUIREMENTS

Interviewer: So, do you understand the fundamental design of the Uber system?

Candidate: I am, of course. But to be more specific, I believe that a few responses from your end can assist me in coming up with a solid system design that meets your needs and scale. Cost-effectiveness can be achieved by all parties in this strategy.

Interview: Sure. Send out your inquiries.

Candidate: So, how exactly should the app function for you? Could you briefly summarize what you hope the app will be able to do?

Interviewer: When a user searches for a cab nearby where they are, our Uber-like app displays all the available cabsm, and calculate the anticipated cab arrival time as well as the anticipated travel time. Additionally, it gives the user an approximate price. The user must, of course, be able to reserve a cab using one of the many payment methods we accept. Once the request is granted, the user and the driver should both be able to track their locations.

Candidate: Great. What are the non-functional requirements?

Interviewer: Our app should be international and operate from any location. As anticipated, latency ought to be very minimal.

If not, users might encounter difficulties locating cabs when they really need them. The system should have high consistency as well as high availability.

Candidate: I'm grateful. I'll have enough information from that to make estimates and give you a complex system design. Give me a few minutes so I can list everything I have to say.

ESTIMATING CONSTRAINTS

Assume that there are 100k active drivers worldwide and 10 million active users using our Uber service.

We require at least 2TB of data to store and cache all of this information using our application servers and a Redis cache server, even if 1M rides are made each day.

To avoid any issues while continuously sending and requesting location information for drivers and customers, it is critical to have at least 1GB/sec bandwidth since all cab drivers must ping the network every five seconds.

MAPS SERVICE

Cab services have existed since the beginning of the industrial revolution. Why is Uber considered so revolutionary? This is due to its capability to direct users to taxis that are already nearby and assist in building a service that connects both of these services. According to the user, Uber also employs cutting-edge machine learning algorithms to select the best driver from the available pool.

So how exactly does Uber accomplish this? Although it is quite complicated, we will make an effort to explain it to you in layman's terms. This idea can be applied to any geolocation service that requires the system to communicate with a specific location.

This method of making and mapping segments will be known as.

Explanation

To better understand the system design from a practical stand-point, let's use New York as an example. Using geographic coordinates, our service should be able to divide the city's geography into various sections. Based on these coordinates, our application can quickly divide a city into sections using any Map API, such as Google Maps.

We can simply assign individual IDs to the segments once they have been divided. Our main goal is to locate a specific taxi's coordinates and connect them to a segment. Utilizing graph algorithms like Dijkstra's algorithm makes this implementation simple.

It's important to keep in mind that because the cabs are typically moving continuously, the segments to which they belong will also be changing. Therefore, it is crucial to continuously ping to the vehicle GPS and track information about which segment they belong to in order to ensure that the coordinate data we have is real-time.

We will use a service, such as "Main Service," for example, to handle all the aforementioned issues.

Multiple tasks will be handled by this "Main Service." To better understand, let's list the primary duties it will be handling:

- Dividing the segments
- Coordinating the handling of these segments and all pings that the service will be sending
- Providing a cab's or a customer's lat/long information and determining which segment they fall under
- Calculating the travel time between two points and providing the driver with a suggested route
- Based on the traffic or requests that segment receives, segmenting or merging. For instance, if Segment 1 experiences heavy traffic and a high volume of customers, the service should be able to split this segment into multiple parts and then match the customer with an appropriate driver. However, if Segment 3 and Segment 4 receive fewer requests, the service should be able to combine them in order to find drivers for the customers.

SYSTEM ARCHITECTURE

Once we are aware of the "Main Service," it is crucial to comprehend how the Uber backend's system architecture actually functions.

Uber typically uses two different apps to interact with customers and drivers.

User App

The user app will be used by all users to communicate with the Uber backend service. A "User Service" that manages all communication will receive all requests before a load balancer, which receives them first. Any system service that can provide information about the user can communicate with this user service. For instance, if a user asks about past trips, the request will first be sent to a load balancer, then to the "User Service," which will then look for the "History Service" that manages the users' past trips and send the user request to "History Service." "History Service" will then send the details about the users' past trips to the "User Service," and the "User Service" will then send the user request back to the user with the aid of user

From a database perspective, MySQL cluster will be used to store all of the user-related data. Redis will be used for all caching.

For instance, when the "User Service" asks for the "History Service," Redis will first send the request to see if any requests have already been cached. In the event that it isn't, the query will be sent to the MySQL database. Once the query has been answered, the response will first be sent to Redis for caching before being sent to the "User Service" to be returned to the user.

When a customer attempts to use Uber to make a cab reservation, they also use a service known as a "Cab Request Service." This service typically establishes a WebSocket connection with the user's device and uses a "Cab Request Service" to display nearby taxis that are available.

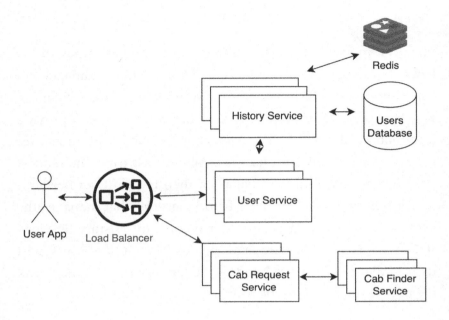

Driver App

When looking for passengers to board their vehicles, all Uber drivers typically use a driver app. The driver app will utilize the same two primary services as the user app in order to fulfill user requests. A load balancer will first be used to process any requests.

The "Driver Service" will be activated whenever the driver needs information about their trips or metadata information such as their details, and it will use MySQL to query the database for the information. Additionally, we can quickly get information from the server and send it back to the driver by using a Redis cache server.

The driver app also has a connection to the "Location Service," which frequently pings the main service to update the segment it is currently in. The segment they are in will change because the driver will be moving continuously.

The user app and driver app will both benefit from a few additional features that will make determining the fare for a ride easier.

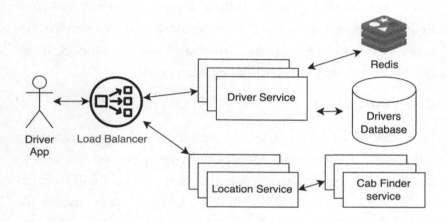

HOW WILL THE CUSTOMERS AND DRIVERS BE LINKED?

The main goal of a service like Uber is to connect users and drivers. We can add a number of additional components to the detailed system design we previously presented to help customers easily find cabs and drivers easily find and select a customer.

Given that the system design is quite intricate, we should approach this issue from two distinct angles.

Customer Component

The customer will establish a WebSocket connection with our web server each time they use the app. Any request made by the user to invoke any service will first go through a load balancer and then land on a random application server.

The customer will typically initiate a service, such as the "Cab Request Service," which will then be connected to a service that locates cabs. In order for the driver and user to connect, a cab finder service should typically be informed of.

Driver Component

Each driver who uses Uber to provide services to customers must open a WebSocket handler with the Uber servers due to the large number of drivers using the app. Drivers will continuously ping their location to the Uber servers using the WebSocket handler, unlike customers who only make one request.

Uber needs to use a WebSocket manager to manage these handlers because there are likely thousands of users with open WebSocket handlers. This manager's role is to serve as a liaison between the driver and the cab-hailing service. Redis or Cassandra can be used to cache all the data as well as the driver's location data. For auditing purposes and to generate the bill based on the driver's actual mileage, location data must be stored.

Cab Finder

The cab finder service will be launched as soon as the customer requests and initiates the "Cab Request Service," and the request will be saved for later consideration. The request will be sent to a WebSocket manager managing the drivers in that specific location based on the customer's coordinates.

The location service and maps service will be activated from the WebSocket manager. The location service will first use the WebSocket handler to ping the driver's location. Once the location information is received, the maps service will segment it and look for customers who have requested cab services.

Thus, all the drivers nearby will be informed when a customer requests a cab finder service. With the aid of a driver priority engine, the Uber algorithms occasionally present you with an alternative strategy.

What Is a Driver Priority Engine?

Drivers won't be instantly associated with a customer. First, a driver priority engine will receive all the driver information after a list of drivers has been gathered from the location. To determine which users are most beneficial to the customer, this engine will now employ ranking algorithms. Finding the right driver for the customer will take into account a number of factors. A regular customer might get the driver who accepts the request first on the app, whereas a premium customer might get the driver with the best reviews.

The "Trip Service" will be activated once a driver has been chosen by the driver priority engine. This service will launch a new interface for the user and the driver after gathering all the information about the user, driver, destination, route, and fare. Additionally, it will generate a personal identification number

(PIN) for each app so that users can authenticate before beginning a ride.

With the help of the "Review Service," users can rate the driver after the ride is over, and they can also leave comments. As soon as the ride is over, all data being pulled up to this point from the MySQL relational database will be immediately sent to Cassandra for future storage purposes.

CHAPTER 9
TIKTOK SYSTEM DESIGN

A well-known social media platform called TikTok shows users short videos. For their already well-known websites, Instagram and YouTube, Google and Facebook have respectively developed new services called Instagram Reels and YouTube Shorts based on the concept of TikTok. TikTok, which uses an algorithm to spread even an unpopular account video to millions of users worldwide, has recently become a cultural phenomenon. Regular users may be encouraged to use the platform more by receiving a large number of views and expressions of support in the form of likes.

From the perspective of system design, the TikTok design is simple to implement and requires few components. However, TikTok uses a lot of resources because the majority of the videos must be kept in the data servers permanently.

UNDERSTANDING REQUIREMENTS

Candidate: I am well-aware of how platforms for social video, like TikTok, are designed. However, being aware of your needs could enable me to improve the system design.

Interviewer: Yes, theoretically the system design should fall somewhere between that of YouTube and Instagram. Users of our service ought to have the ability to upload videos, and users ought to have access to all other users' videos in their feeds. It is recommended that only brief videos be uploaded.

Candidate: What about non-functional requirements?

Interviewer: Due to the high demand for these services today, the system should be highly available and scalable. The user shouldn't experience any lag while using the application, and latency should also be low. Eventual consistency is acceptable, and it's perfectly normal if users can't access the video right away.

ESTIMATIONS

Let's assume that the system has 10 million active users and that 100 thousand videos are uploaded each day.

We might need 5MB per video because the majority of our videos are short.

100,000 * 5 MB = 500 GB

Therefore, on a distributed storage, we require at least 500GB of data daily that is set aside specifically for the storage of videos.

A separate database should also be used to store all other metadata data. We might require at least 5GB per day for this.

We might require a bandwidth of at least 6MB/sec because we will be dealing with at least 500GB of database transfer per day, on average.

500 GB / 86,400 =5 MB/sec

OVERALL SYSTEM DESIGN

TikTok is a mobile application, so browsers typically do not support it. Additionally, we'll try to create a system that only supports iOS and Android devices.

Client

The client will attempt to use a tablet or mobile device to access the service, and they will send requests to the application servers. A load balancer usually handles all of the requests made by the users. The main servers will experience a decrease in workload and an increase in availability thanks to the load balancer.

Upload Service

Our TikTok system design is not complete without the ability to upload videos. The videos are not as large as those on YouTube because the platform only supports videos between 20 and 30 seconds in length. We will significantly reduce our storage and bandwidth costs as a result.

So, whenever a user tries to upload a video, the load balancer will immediately send it to the "Upload Service." The video can now be uploaded using this service to a database or a different distributed storage. It is advised to store all the metadata in an RDBMS, such as NoSQL or MySQL, for better latency.

It is a good idea to develop a separate distribution system to store all the videos if the service needs to be more scalable. Therefore, after the upload service starts, the videos should first be processed using a distributed queue before being stored in a distributed system. Several tasks may need to be completed on a video that is being uploaded by the user in a distributed queue:

- The authenticity of the videos can be automatically verified by using a content verification service. We can automatically find and remove any duplicate or violently explicit videos.
- Before sending the video back to the distributed storage, we can split it into a number of smaller pieces using video splitter algorithms. Splitting makes the video file smaller, making it easier to store.
- Encoding methods allow us to change the format of video.

For instance, if you upload a video from an Android device, it will have its own format. However, if you open the video on an iPad, the encoding mechanism will take control and give you an iPad-compatible version of the video.

We need to figure out a way to guarantee that these videos will show up on the user's feed after they are uploaded to our database storage.

· · ·

Video Feed Service

The primary user interface (UI) that users see when they first launch the app is the TikTok news feed. It resembles a Facebook news feed or a Twitter timeline quite a bit. The news feed in TikTok, however, will only contain brief videos.

From the standpoint of system design, you must push videos from followers or celebrities to the user's news feed. TikTok also makes use of random algorithms to show well-liked trending videos.

A video will therefore be sent to a distributed storage after being uploaded and encoded using the distributed queue. However, the video will be processed through a feed generator before being sent to the storage. A feed generator is a system component that searches all users who follow a specific ID for the UserID associated with the video that is being uploaded.

The uploaded video will then be preloaded into a few users' feeds and a distributed cache system will be created. Only a few posts are initially stored in each distributed cache, but as soon as the user requests a refresh, a push request is sent to the servers, and new posts from other users begin to appear on the feed. Every user in this system will have access to the distributed cache, making things simple.

We must integrate a CDN into the system after determining the logic for the upload and feed services.

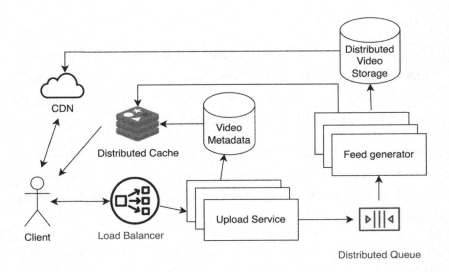

CONTENT DELIVERY NETWORK

Videos of well-known celebrities who have a large following and consequently more views are frequently delivered via CDN. Popular videos may occasionally lag if the service must constantly pull the video from distributed storage due to the volume of requests that must be handled by the service.

We need a service that will push these popular videos directly to the CDN in order to reach as many users as possible in order to deliver them quickly.

DATABASE TABLE SCHEMA

The database schema can help us in comprehending how uploaded content and metadata can be retrieved for the user and displayed in accordance with their requests.

· · ·

Video Metadata Table

- UserID - User account identifier.
- VideoID - Unique identifier for every video uploaded to the platform.
- VideoURL - Every video that is uploaded to the platform will have a different URL created for it. Simply sharing this will allow users to watch the video on their app or browser.
- Status - Information about the state of the video, such as whether it has been uploaded or verified, will be provided using this.
- Description - Users typically type this brief passage of text while uploading the video.
- VideoCategory - The category that the video might fall under is included in this metadata information. This is an option that users will have when uploading a video.
- LikesCount - The likes for a video will be calculated using this auto-incremented value.

Video Comment Table

- VideoID - Distinct ID for each uploaded video.
- CommentID - Unique ID for a comment.
- Comment - The text of comment.

It is possible to query database operations using any of the database schema that we have previously described. We can also make use of a cache database, such as Redis, as it is frequently challenging to retrieve data directly from an RDBMS database.

WHAT WILL CACHE DATABASE DO?

The process of creating a TikTok news feed typically involves downloading videos from a distributed cache or storage. It takes longer to query information from these databases because the metadata data is typically stored in an RDBMS.

Redis will be used to make it simple to access metadata data for a specific user. When a user asks for a video to be added to their news feed, the application server first sends the request to a Redis cache server to see if any videos related to the user already exist. If there are videos, it is referred to as a "Cache Hit," and the users' news feed will display the videos right away. When there are no videos, the situation is known as a "Cache Miss," and because the server does not have any videos or metadata, the request is sent to the database, where the content is then retrieved. All of the data will be saved in the Redis server once it has been retrieved.

CONCLUSION

We want to start by congratulating you on finishing this book. It's a hard subject, so we're happy you persevered through it to the end. Being an expert in system design is a lifelong endeavor, and we have no doubt that you will create some ground-breaking systems for various services all over the world.

Here are a few more pointers before you go that will help you successfully complete your System Design interviews:

1. Always start simple, then get more complicated.

Users are advised to begin their interview for any service or website by first outlining the system's surface areas. You can introduce complex elements of the design once the interviewer starts paying attention as a result of simplicity. Due to the simplicity of the components and the short preparation time, this strategy will also enable you to have a fruitful conversation with the interviewer.

2. Explain your procedure.

You are completely free to approach the issue however you choose in an interview. However, you must explain to the interviewer why you chose the particular process. While explaining the rationale, all of your choices should make sense to the interviewer.

3. Interviewers may confuse you.

The deliberate letting of candidates go in the wrong direction during an interview is one of the many gimmicks interviewers use on them. Never alter your system design or take their claims at face value. Don't let the interviewer dictate your system design because it should ultimately be yours. However, if you have any genuine questions, you can approach them and get their advice.

4. Draw architectural diagrams.

It is advised that you hand-draw diagrams prior to an interview in order to better express your ideas.

5. Be confident.

Being confident is crucial when participating in interviews. Mention every concern the interviewers have expressed and confidently address it.

We hope your career as a system design professional is successful.

I'd like to hear from you and hope that you could take some time to post a review on Amazon. Your feedback and support will help this author to greatly improve his writing craft for future projects and make this book even better.

I want you, the reader, to know that your review is very important and so, if you'd like to leave a review, all you have to do is to scan the QR code and away you go.

REFERENCES

Designing Instagram - Grokking the System Design Interview. (n.d.). Educative: Interactive Courses for Software Developers. https://www.educative.io/courses/grokking-the-system-design-interview/m2yDVZnQ8lG

L, N. (2018, September 8). *System design for Twitter.* Medium. https://medium.com/@narengowda/system-design-for-twitter-e737284afc95

srivastava, J. (2020, December 21). *Dating Application System Design. System Design Concepts.* https://medium.com/system-design-concepts/dating-application-system-design-aae411412267

System Design Tutorial. (2021, July 14). GeeksforGeeks. https://www.geeksforgeeks.org/system-design-tutorial/

System Design of Uber App - Uber System Architecture. (2020, November 20). GeeksforGeeks. https://www.geeksforgeeks.org/system-design-of-uber-app-uber-system-architecture/